UNDERSTANDING REVELATION

UNDERSTANDING REVELATION

PREPARING BELIEVERS FOR THEIR COMING KING

WRITTEN BY

MALCOLM HEDDING

Published by Intend Publishing
1921 New Salem Road, Hwy. 99
Murfreesboro, TN 37128

ISBN 978-1-61718-007-1
ISBN 978-1-61718-023-1 (electronic)

CONTENTS

COMMENDATIONS

Here is a 'must read' written by Malcolm Hedding in his usual energetic and clear style. His book on John's Revelation is to the point and very practical for Christian life in a challenging world. For preachers of the Gospel: This book will give you a good lead into Revelation and inspiration to preach on it.

Dr. Charles P. Watt
South Africa

Malcolm Hedding has a unique gifting both as a teacher and as a speaker. He does teach as one who has (divine) authority with a ministry which is respected both within Christian and Jewish circles. He has the ability to take profound truths and express them in a clear, understandable style.

Sadly, today there are few teachers of historic premillennialism. This was the prevalent view of the early church until the Council of Ephesus in AD 431. Historic

pre-millennialism sees from Scripture, a coming Messianic kingdom which is inextricably linked to the land and the people of Israel. Such a view is known as Biblical or Christian Zionism.

Malcolm is an international exponent of both historic pre-millennialism and Biblical Zionism.

This devotional and insightful commentary on Revelation is a must read book for all who long for the blessed hope of the appearing of our great God and Saviour Jesus Christ.

Dr. David Elms

United Kingdom

FORWARD

Malcolm Hedding represents a unique collection of experience. He was a pastor in South Africa challenging an apartheid state. He served as the executive director of the International Christian Embassy in Jerusalem for many years. He worked with Israeli political leaders, welcomed leaders from around the world to Jerusalem and traveled the globe speaking to churches and gatherings of Christians. He knows firsthand the challenges of the 21st century Church in the earth. His wealth of experience provides a unique perspective in understanding and teaching the Word of God.

The Book of Revelation is often polarizing. Many choose to avoid the work altogether, declaring it to be unknowable or intimidating. Others maintain a fascination with the images and characters of the prophetic pictures of Revelation.

Malcolm provides a remarkable perspective on the Book of Revelation. He invites the reader into the text, providing a devotional approach to the truth presented. His insights help illuminate the promises and warnings of

God. His combination of scholarship and pastoral concern are very helpful in sorting through the complexities of Revelation and therefore his discussion of the "temporal, eternal and eschatological" aspects of Revelation constitutes very helpful distinctions. Malcolm does a remarkable job of introducing the reader to Jesus throughout the Book of Revelation. It is after all a "Revelation of Jesus Christ."

For those who have stood apart from the Book of Revelation, this book provides a wonderful invitation to know our Lord as King. For the person who has invested much in the study of Revelation, Malcolm provides a wealth of insight and understanding. As you read, I pray the Lord will open the eyes of your understanding. I thank my friend for his efforts in study and writing to provide such a powerful tool for the Body of Christ.

G. Allen Jackson

Senior Pastor of World Outreach Church

Murfreesboro, Tennessee, USA

PREFACE

The Revelation of Jesus Christ, which God gave Him to show His servants–things which must shortly take place. And He sent and signified it by His angel to His servant John, who bore witness to the word of God, and to the testimony of Jesus Christ, to all things that he saw.

Revelation 1:1-2

The Book of Revelation has supremely to do with the unveiling of Jesus. That is; a Church in the world plagued by wealth, compromise, and slumber needs to see Jesus afresh. There is no more urgent need! The Church in general must awaken or die and be rejected by Christ. He said:

"I know your works, that you have a name that you are alive, but you are dead. Be watchful, and strengthen the things which remain, that are ready to die, for I have not found your works perfect before God."

Revelation 3:1-2

Thus it is that the first three chapters of the Book dwell on this pressing theme. However, the main body of

the Book lays emphasis on the sovereignty of God, His redemptive initiative, and that which must take place on earth in order for Jesus to be physically and visibly revealed to a rebellious and dying world. The fruit of wickedness must be brought to ripeness, meaning that iniquity must be brought forth into the open, demanding the return of Jesus to deal with it. This in turn means that as we approach the end of the age, conditions on earth will become more complex, dangerous, and severe. These conditions are likened in the Bible to birth pangs that come upon a woman ready to give birth. These become more intense and severe as the time of deliverance draws near. In the same way, conditions on the earth will worsen in all respects before God, by Jesus Christ, brings forth His visible kingdom on the Earth.

Indeed, such will be the conditions on earth that, according to scripture, men's hearts will fail them (Luke 21:26). I believe that these days are fast approaching and, in fact, are already here in some respects! The warnings of the Book of Revelation must therefore be taken quite seriously. Sadly, much of the wider Church has ignored and, quite frankly, rejected the Book as being too complicated and difficult to understand. They have done this to their peril. Others find the Book too embarrassing; the contents of its pages are so fantastic that to believe in them makes them

feel foolish. These readers forget that the ways of God always contradict the ways of the world and its thinking (Isaiah 55:8-9). Indeed, God's wisdom and knowledge are considered foolish by the world, and we must be prepared to bear this reproach (1 Corinthians 1:20-21). Those who live in the fear and respect of men will never know God!

In some respects, our views of the Book of Revelation are a reflection of what we are. No wonder a blessing is reserved for those who read it and heed its warnings.

> *Blessed is he who reads and those who hear the words of this prophecy, and keep those things which are written in it; for the time is near.*
>
> Revelation 1:3

Once again it must be stressed that the Book of Revelation is chiefly about the visible, real second coming of Jesus. This is the blessed hope of the Church (Titus 2:11-13) and the people of God everywhere are in urgent need of rekindling this hope. Jesus told a parable about ten virgins, which is recorded in the twenty-fifth chapter of Matthew. Five were ready and prepared for their Lord's coming, but five were sleepy and reckless. Suddenly the Bridegroom came, and before they could recover appropriately to greet

him they were shut out of the great marriage banquet. This will be the conditions prevailing on the earth when Jesus comes again. The Church will be weighed down with neglect and complacency, and the Book of Revelation is "designed" to rectify these spiritual failures and prepare the people of God for Christ's return. More than ever, the Book of Revelation must be opened by and to the Church.

So many consider its pages difficult to understand, but the truth is they are not! Much of the information in the Book is found in the Hebrew scriptures of Genesis, Exodus, Daniel, and Zechariah. Once this principle is known, the Book opens like a flower for all to behold its truth and its beauty. Because it is a magnificent volume. After all, it must be remembered that the Book is addressed to the Church in the world and not to the millions of people who have rejected Christ and His kingdom. The idea that three quarters of the Book (chapters 6 through 19) does not apply to the Church is just nonsense!

This is a recent idea that essentially removes the message of Jesus in the Book from His Church. Naturally, the reasons for doing this are all set forth in spiritual language, but they remain nevertheless wrong and, I believe, displease our Lord greatly. The truth is, the whole Book is for the whole Body of Christ! We should be careful—yes, very

careful—about removing its relevance to the people of God. Jesus made a very serious warning about this:

> *For I testify to everyone who hears the words of the prophecy of this book: If anyone adds to these things, God will add to him the plagues that are written in this book; and if anyone takes away from the words of the book of this prophecy, God shall take away his part from the Book of Life, from the holy city, and from the things which are written in this book.*
>
> Revelation 22:18-19

I therefore encourage you to spend much time in this Book, because now is the time to understand its message. What you don't understand, simply pass over, but keep reading it time and time again, and do so with complete reliance upon the Holy Spirit to help you see more clearly as He illuminates its pages with light from Heaven. Those who give themselves to this holy work will be enriched beyond measure. This has been my experience, and I know that it will be yours as well. As you finally close the Book you will be able to agree with the Spirit of God by saying, "Even so, Lord Jesus come!"

Malcolm Hedding

CHAPTER ONE
THE STAGE

Then I turned to see the voice that spoke with me. And having turned I saw seven golden lampstands, and in the midst of the seven lampstands One like the Son of Man, clothed with a garment down to the feet and girded about the chest with a golden band.

Revelation 1:12-13

OUR WORLD

The unveiling of Jesus is what the Book of Revelation is all about. It is much like a theatre on Broadway in New York or in the West End of London: when everything is set onstage and the audience is seated, the curtain goes up and the main actors are

seen and revealed for who they are. This is the idea behind the Book of Revelation. Our world, and indeed history, has not been abandoned to the forces of chaos, evil, confusion, and chance (evolution), although this is precisely what the Devil and his hordes want you to believe.

On the contrary, the world is being made ready, through judgment, for the physical and visible manifestation of Jesus. Once everything "in the theatre" is in place, He will step onto the stage of history for all to see, even those who pierced Him!

> *Behold, He is coming with clouds, and every eye will see Him, even they who pierced Him. And all the tribes of the earth will mourn because of Him. Even so, Amen.*
>
> Revelation 1:7

This judgment to which the world is being brought will also burn in the Church. For the world, this judgment is physical—that is, Jesus warned of earthquakes, wars, plagues, natural upheavals, and disease that will ravage the world just before He comes again. However, for the Church this judgment is spiritual and breaks out before His judgment on the world escalates. The Apostle Peter reminds us that God's judgment and correction begins with

the household of God (1Peter 4:17).

JESUS AND HIS PEOPLE

The first chapter of the Book of Revelation centers in on the spiritual unveiling or revelation of Christ. John is "in the Spirit on the Lord's Day" and is consequently swept up into a magnificent picture of Jesus. So overwhelming is it that he falls in dismay before His feet and is subsequently told to take a crucial message to the seven churches of Asia by means of a written manuscript.

> *...saying, "I am the Alpha and the Omega, the First and the Last," and, "What you see, write in a book and send it to the seven churches which are in Asia: to Ephesus, to Smyrna, to Pergamos, to Thyatira, to Sardis, to Philadelphia, and to Laodicea."*
>
> Revelation 1:11

This amazing picture of Jesus embodies the qualities that the Church in the world should embrace in order to be spiritually healthy. So the failures of the local church are corrected by repentance and appropriation of an aspect of His person that they have thus far failed to see or have abandoned. (Compare Revelation 12:12 with Revelation

1:16 and Revelation 2:1 with Revelation 1:16.) The message is therefore clear: Jesus is the center and at the center of everything. John sees Him in the midst of seven golden candlesticks. Moreover, the churches are also obligated to reflect Him to a dying, broken, and lost world. Jesus reaches our dark world through His people, and this means that when the world sees us it should see enough of Jesus to be amazed. The antagonists of the early church recognized the reality of Jesus in the lives of His Disciples and marveled (Acts 4:13).

I well remember a gold plaque affixed to a pulpit of a church in such a way that it "greeted" the preacher with these words, "Sir, we would see Jesus." How true! This is what it means to be "Jesus' Folk" as one preacher friend of mine puts it. We are to reflect Jesus and it is vital that Jesus' Folk embrace this challenge and master it by God's grace. Paul said, "Follow me as I follow Christ." Another preacher friend of mine talks about cooperating with the Sprit of God in such a way that Christ is formed in us. Those who learn to cooperate with the grace of God will meet Christ visibly in the air when He comes, not in wrath, but in glorification. Paul describes this glorious day thus:

...and to give you who are troubled rest with us when

the Lord Jesus is revealed from heaven with His mighty angels, in flaming fire taking vengeance on those who do not know God, and on those who do not obey the gospel of our Lord Jesus Christ. These shall be punished with everlasting destruction from the presence of the Lord and from the glory of His power, when He comes, in that Day, to be glorified in His saints and to be admired among all those who believe, because our testimony among you was believed.

2 Thessalonians 1:7-10

These faithful ones so gloriously raptured to meet the Lord in the air as He comes to judge the ungodly will hear the long expected and beautiful refrain, "The kingdoms of this world have become the kingdoms of the Lord and of His Christ..." (Revelation 11:15)

THE MESSAGE

The message of chapter one is that we are called to appropriate Christ in His fullness, nothing more and nothing less. Moreover, there will be no appropriation of His fullness, apart from being willing to travel the road of suffering. This remains a very unpopular message but it is nevertheless true; Jesus' face is glorious but His feet are

of "burnished bronze." That is, Scripture speaks about the testing, correction, and judgment of believers. John saw Christ so fully because he was a prisoner on the island of Patmos and a "companion in the tribulation and kingdom and patience of Jesus Christ" (Revelation 1:9).

Paul reminded Christ's followers that through many tribulations we enter into the kingdom of God (Acts 14:22), and Jesus told His people at the church of Smyrna, "Do not fear any of those things which you are about to suffer" (Revelation 2:10). We cannot avoid the way of the cross, though many try!

THE OUTLINE OF REVELATION

John hears a voice calling upon him to write down the things he has seen, the things that are, and the things that will take place after these things (Revelation 1:9). In other words, John is to write about the following:

- The things temporal—Chapters 1-3; 22:6-21.
- The things eternal—Chapters 4-5.
- The things eschatological—Chapters 6-22:1-5.

CHAPTER TWO

SPECIAL DEVOTION

The Judgment of Believers

THE INESCAPABLE FUTURE

Every believer in Christ will, in the end, appear before the judgment seat of Jesus. This is certain and inescapable! Paul refers to this reality a few times in his epistles:

But why do you judge your brother? Or why do you show contempt for your brother? For we shall all stand before the judgment seat of Christ. For it is written:

"As I live, says the Lord, every knee shall bow to me, and every tongue shall confess to God." So then each of us shall give account of himself to God.

Romans 14:10-12

And:

For we must all appear before the judgment seat of Christ, that each one may receive the things done in the body, according to what he has done, whether good or bad.

2 Corinthians 5:10

This awesome day will not determine whether we can enter heaven or not. No, it will determine the truth about our walk with Jesus, while we lived on earth, and what reward or rather "station" we will occupy in eternity. Again, Paul writes:

Each one's work will become clear; for the Day will declare it, because it will be revealed by fire; and the fire will test each one's work, of what sort it is. If anyone's work which he has built on it endures, he will receive a reward. If anyone's work is burned, he will suffer loss; but he himself will be saved, yet so as through fire.

1 Corinthians 3:13-15

However, God judges His people now! By this process, which is also inescapable, He purifies His people and sanctifies them.

PAUL'S THEOLOGY

Paul addresses this issue more fully in 2 Thessalonians, chapter 1. Here he tells us that God's judgment over the Christ follower is internal, external, and ironic.

Internal

...so that we ourselves boast of you among the churches of God for your patience and faith in all your persecutions and tribulations that you endure, which is manifest evidence of the righteous judgment of God, that you may be counted worthy of the kingdom of God, for which you also suffer...

2 Thessalonians 1:4-5

That is, by judgment we are "cleaned up" and made to approximate more fully the image of Jesus. On the cross, Jesus dealt with our sins by dying for them, but by His resurrection, and thus life within us, He deals with our sin (Romans 5:10). Original or besetting sin is not easily removed from our lives, so from time to time, the Lord has to judge us to remove it. As we endure, we are counted worthy of the Kingdom of God for which, indeed, we suffer. Peter writes that sometimes this process can be quite bewildering,

as we cannot fully understand it (1 Peter 4:12). We must persevere because we are convinced about the righteous, pure, and loving character of God. Sometimes we do not have to understand, all we need to do is hold His hand!

External

...that you may be counted worthy of the kingdom of God, for which you also suffer.

2 Thessalonians 1:5

Our destiny is Heaven, our home is Heaven, our goal is Heaven and our redemption is with Heaven in mind. The process of judgment, through which we shall all pass as believers, is designed to keep us focused with our spiritual gaze upon the eternal realm of Heaven. When we set our focus upon our real future we get our priorities right and become more Christ-like (Colossians 3:1-4; Hebrews 12:1-2).

Ironic

...since it is a righteous thing with God to repay with tribulation those who trouble you.

2 Thessalonians 2:6

That is, the people prepared for hell are the people God will use to prepare you for Heaven! We work with these people, live with them in our communities, and interact with them in all spheres of human endeavor. God does not change them; no, He uses them to change us! Years ago I found myself working in a huge glass manufacturing factory that employed some thirteen thousand people. I was in the financial department, and to my amazement, the people who worked in this office were "from hell"! I was a young believer in Jesus, and I quickly realized that if I was going to survive, I would have to endure their hostility and stand up for my faith in Jesus.

This was a very difficult time for me, but I knew without a doubt that God had put me there, and today I thank God for it, since these ungodly people strengthened my faith and thereby made a wonderful contribution to my walk with Jesus. The people prepared for hell prepared me for heaven! What a blessing. This is truly ironic, but happy are those who have been trained by this process of judgment. It is certainly not pleasant at the time but it does yield the peaceable fruit of righteousness (1 Peter 4:1-2; Hebrews 12:11).

We all need our faith in Jesus to be strengthened, firmed up, and enlarged, as this will enable us to

unashamedly stand up for Jesus. Only the process of God's loving judgment can achieve this in our lives. There is no shortcut to spiritual maturity, and we must all remember that important as Bible reading, prayer and fellowship are there is still no substitute for the strange ways of God. If we know God and are convinced that He is good and disciplines us only for our best interests, we will trust Him fully and patiently submit ourselves to the season of judgment and correction.

THE THINGS TEMPORAL

CHAPTER THREE

THE MESSAGE OF JESUS TO THE SEVEN CHURCHES OF ASIA

"I am the Alpha and the Omega, the first and the Last," and, "What you see write in a book and send it to the seven churches which are in Asia..."

Revelation 1:11

THE LOCAL CHURCH

The seven churches of Asia are the immediate focus of Jesus' attention. They "house" His people, are temples of the Holy Spirit, and are the instruments by which He pursues His work on earth. Moreover, the local church is the expression of His presence and purpose on earth. It is also worth noting that one is a

member of the universal Church to the extent that one is a member of the local Church. Christians who fall around belonging nowhere are living in contradiction of Scripture. Christians should and must be in a community, since God, by His Spirit, does not commit all of His gifts to one person, no matter how spiritual or qualified. We are deceived if we think we can get by on our own because we have enough of Jesus.

It is only as we come together in community that we can fully experience the life of Jesus. Our unity is always in diversity (1 Corinthians 12:5-6), and as we worship and serve together, we enjoy a fuller understanding of who Christ is. Paul writes that the redemptive work of God in Christ has baptized us (placed us all) into the one body of Jesus and caused us to "drink" of the Spirit of God.

> *For as the body is one and has many members, but all the members of that one body, being many, are one body, so also is Christ. For by one Spirit we were all baptized into one body—whether Jews or Greeks, whether slaves or free—and have all been made to drink of one Spirit.*
>
> 1 Corinthians 12:12-13

There is thus a manifestation of the Spirit of God in

the assembled body of Jesus that you cannot appropriate on your own. This, in itself, is good reason why we should not neglect our local church attendance. To be faithful in this regard requires discipline and dedication, and God definitely expects these of us. (Hebrews 10:19-25)

THE SEVEN CHURCHES OF ASIA

Having drawn attention to the above, it is important to understand what the seven churches of Asia represent:

They were real historical churches. They would have been "set in order" (Titus 1:5) with "Ephesian four" gift ministries, elders, and deacons. Their struggles, problems, triumphs, and blessings were no different from that of local churches today. Jesus is therefore addressing real followers in real time!

They can be seen as a reflection of the state of the church through the centuries to the present. The similarities between each church in sequence and that of the historical journey of the Church through two thousand years are far too amazing and uncanny to be a mere coincidence.

So the loveless church of Ephesians (Revelation 2:1-7)

is a picture of the second-century Church. It still had purity of doctrine and good order, but it was descending into formality and ritual that no longer served the presence of Jesus. In short, they were losing their "first love" and becoming religious! Only a vibrant and burning love for Jesus can remedy this spiritual malady that has always threatened and infected God's people. There is only one answer: repentance.

The church of Smyrna (Revelation 2:8-11) is most certainly the suffering Church of the middle second, third, and fourth centuries: a church subjected to persecution and thus one of sorrows and tribulation but, nevertheless, a faithful church. Jesus does not call them to repentance, but to faithfulness, and He reminds them that even in imprisonment and death they have nothing to fear if they follow Him. This reflects the triumph of the Gospel.

By contrast, the church of Pergamos (Revelation 2:12-17) is moving away from the simple structure and liturgy upon which the "beginning church" was built. It is thus on the way to status, hierarchy, and compromise. Here we have a picture of the Church from the fifth to the ninth century. It is a compromising church, but nevertheless it has some strength in that it can dwell where "Satan's throne" is. This was a huge temple-type structure that was built in honor

of Zeus or Jupiter. Today you can see much of this original structure in Berlin. The believer Antipas withstood this demonic onslaught and became a martyr. Antipas means "against everything." Sometimes the world around us, and even the Church, is so corrupt and dark that we have to be against everything in order to survive spiritually.

This period witnessed the church gaining much earthly power, prestige, and influence, but at the same time, losing much heavenly power and blessing. To the world it was a shining jewel, having conquered the then known world, but to Jesus it was filled with idolatry, immorality, and manipulation. It needed to repent!

From the tenth through the fourteenth century, the church forsook its birthright, departed from biblical truth, and plunged into darkness. This was a thoroughly corrupt church void of the presence and power of God. The church at Thyatira (Revelation 2:18-29) was filled with sexual impurity and evil. Even the "deep things of Satan" had infiltrated the church. Herein most certainly is a warning to all of us today. The "gates of the church" must be protected by prayer and watchfulness, for if they are not, the Devil himself can get inside! This is a very sad testimony, as it brings the fair name of Jesus into disrepute. This saga has been repeated time and again through the centuries. Even today,

great movements of God have choked and fallen because of the inroads that have been set up by the powers of darkness. It will not stop; we must be watchful and repentant.

The fifteenth-century Church saw the beginnings of renewal. This is the period of the Reformation. It is important to note that Martin Luther's work and ministry was more foundational than it was reviving. It was, however, important to a lay a good theological foundation before a "new house" could be built upon it. So Jesus addresses the dead church of Sardis (Revelation 3:1-6). He says, "you have a name that you are alive, but you are dead." Luther courageously swept away the dead debris of false doctrine that had completely removed the truth of the Gospel from the common people. Justification by faith was again rediscovered and restored to be the centerpiece of biblical proclamation. A new day had come to the people of God, and they were emerging out of spiritual darkness. Millions were ultimately impacted as the fire of the Reformation took hold in Europe and beyond.

However, not all was well within the precincts of the reforming Church. Its reputation was one of spiritual life. But death, that is, spiritual death, still permeated its sanctuaries, and still more fateful was the fact that Luther allowed himself to be deceived by the spirit of anti-Semitism. He

thus sowed destructive "seeds" that would eventually grow into trees of hatred against the Jewish people. The fruit of these trees were taken by Hitler and his thugs and used to murder six million Jews in the twentieth century.

Nevertheless, Luther brought new hope and revived a message that truly saves. Change was underway and the risen Christ was again renewing His Church. This process began to impact the world, and by the eighteenth century, new foundations had been laid upon which the Holy Spirit could build. True revival was coming!

In the eighteenth and nineteenth centuries, three amazing things happened. First, God breathed life into a waiting Church. Second, a great missionary endeavor was launched that covered much of the globe, and third, a movement began within the hearts of the Jews that called them back to Zion and the promised land of Canaan. The church of Philadelphia had arrived (Revelation 3:7-13).

This church held a special place in the heart of God, who, by Christ Jesus, opened up an effective door of service for it. It is certainly no coincidence that this period witnessed the greatest revival the world has seen thus far. The brothers John and Charles Wesley, together with George Whitfield, set a fire ablaze in Britain, and beyond that swept countless millions into the Kingdom of God. Their

message was biblical, sound, unpopular, but very effective in the "hands" of the Holy Spirit. It was evangelical in the true sense of the word, in that it used God's Law to drive people to the cross of Jesus for salvation and forgiveness. They knew that the Holy Spirit could only convict the heart of sin if sin was properly defined. For them sin was violating God's character as it is reflected in the Ten Commandments. They truly knew that the Law is a "tutor to bring us to Christ" and that by "the law is the knowledge of sin" (Galatians 3:24; Romans 3:20). Because of this way of preaching, they became known as the people of the method. Hence they were later called Methodists.

I dare say that if they preached in many of our churches today, they would be removed on the grounds that they were far too direct, offensive, and intolerant. Sermons on hell, death, and sin are not welcomed today, since they offend the carnal sensibilities of God-hating churchgoers!

The twentieth and twenty-first centuries have witnessed a great apostasy on one hand and a remnant Church on the other hand, embracing truth and renewal. Great Church movements have abandoned the true Gospel of Jesus with its call to repentance followed by faith in the finished work of Jesus on the cross. Liberation theology, urban theology, and social justice theology have become the

preferred options. The Church has also followed the lead of the ungodly secular world by embracing as acceptable deviant forms of sexual behavior and "strange flesh" concepts of marriage. What God clearly intended for a man and a woman in marriage has been joyously overthrown, and thus the biblical concept of marriage and family, which has undergirded society for four thousand years, has been attacked and devalued. Truly the lukewarm church of Laodicea has arrived (Revelation 3:14-22).

Bible-believing Christians are being demonized as bigots, and the "new church" happily attacks the inspiration of Scripture and its truth and seeks to delegitimize Christians who believe that Jesus is the only way of salvation. And, if this is not enough, this apostate lukewarm church has forged strong alliances with Islamic groups in order to dismantle the state of Israel. Jesus will vomit them out of His mouth if they do not repent, because they have left Him on the outside looking in and He is calling them to think again and let Him in. They are wretched, miserable, blind, spiritually poor, and truly naked, but they don't even know it! May God help us not to walk in its ways.

The Churches of Asia send a message about the uniqueness of the Body of Christ. That Jesus takes time to

address a church that in general is failing and imperfect is amazing. This goes to show the depth of His grace, because in all these churches is a remnant true and faithful to Him. This gives us an idea of the uniqueness of the local Church and the dignity that Jesus affords it. It is the "house of His presence," and therefore the human stones that make up this house are precious because He lives in them (1 Peter 2:4-5). The lesson is clear—the way we treat one another is the way we treat Jesus! We should never forget this, and this is precisely why Paul said that no longer do we know anybody "according to the flesh," or as mere human beings (2 Corinthians 5:16).

The local Church is thus more than a meeting place. It is the vibrant and real life of Christ on earth. When we forget this, we devalue the Church and rob the people of God of their God-given dignity. Many in the modern Church are guilty of this sin.

The seven churches of Asia provide a picture of the type of Church that Jesus desires and longs for. A composite examination of all the churches of Asia and especially of that which pleases Jesus will demonstrate or reveal the type of church that Jesus desires. It is important to note that His desire is not for perfection, for He knows that this

is beyond the people of God. What He desires is a heart attitude that longs to please Him in every way (Colossians 1:9-10, 1 Thessalonians 2:4). Anything short of this is simply not good enough. Repentance is something that begins with conviction of the heart, and where it is genuine it leads to real change and overcoming.

Thus the answer to each of the churches' failures reflected in these pages is to embrace an aspect of Jesus as seen by John in chapter one. This "forgotten part of Jesus," if grasped with a genuine heart's desire and repentance, will rectify the spiritual malady being addressed. Therefore, to the corrupt church of Thyatira Jesus says, "These things says the Son of God, who has eyes like a flame of fire and His feet like fine brass" (Revelation 1:14-15; Revelation 2:18). They had forgotten that He was holy and will judge His people if they turn to wickedness. They needed to see Jesus again and, if the truth be known, we all need to see Jesus all the time (Hebrews 12:1-2). When we truly see His glory, through prayer and prayerful study of His word, we continue to be transformed into this likeness by His Spirit. Christians fail when they stop looking! The chapters in question then give us a list of the things that creep into our lives when we no longer see Jesus with the eye of faith. The list might be a short one, but it is a very dangerous and

serious one.

Jesus warns about the local church being of the world and not in the world. That is, it reflects the values of a lost and dying world and not those of the Kingdom of God. Worldliness is actually a matter of the heart, because anything that supplants the supreme place that Jesus should hold in your life is worldliness. We must not "love the world." The snare in this regard is always the same; the lust of the eyes, the lust of the flesh, and the boastful pride of life, or the desire for things, the desire for gratification, and the desire for importance (1 John 2:15-17). All of these, which can appear to be quite legitimate, must be brought into subjection to Christ.

Then Jesus has a concern about churches that are being led by "spiritual tyrants." He constantly refers to the "doctrine of the Nicolatians." The word nicolatians means "power over the laity." To put it bluntly, He is referring to leaders who use their position in the local Church to exploit the people of God (Revelation 2:6, 15). The way preachers abuse their congregations to get money out of them today is awful to say the least. I recently watched a preacher on TV who promised each and every donor who sent in a donation to his ministry a personal prophetic word from God! Sadly, many of "God's sheep" do it. This is because people trust

the man of God; when he tells them to empty their wallets because God told him that they have to do this, they believe him! Because they fear God they are easily exploited and manipulated, even more so because they are promised financial reward for doing so. Jesus hates this! It is shameful and always ends up bringing His fair name into disrepute.

Jesus is also concerned about the matter of deception. He laments the fact that "false apostles" have infiltrated the local church in order to use spiritual gifts to obtain status, wealth, and position. In other words the "doctrine of Balaam" has deceived the people of God. Balaam was a true prophet of God, but he was quite prepared to employ his remarkable prophetic gift to obtain prestige and money. Jesus also hates this (Revelation 2:14). Again, this sin is everywhere in the Church today. I was recently told about a preacher of great renown who was earning $150,000 a month—not in America, but in a country that we would generally describe as poor!

And then there is the sad but ongoing problem of sexual impurity. Time and time again, Jesus refers to this problem (Revelation 2:14, 20, 22). Not much has changed over the centuries; today we are plagued by this type of sin that tears the work of God down and makes it a laughing stock in the world. Worse still is the fact that vast parts of

the so-called confessing Church are giving the stamp of divine approval upon perverted sexual behavior! Gay relationships are now accepted as normal even though the Bible condemns them and has always sanctified marriage as an institution reserved for a man and a woman (Romans 1:21-27).

Finally, the Church is guilty of being deaf. The constant refrain that one reads in Jesus' message to the seven churches of Asia is, "He that has an ear, let him hear what the Spirit says to the churches" (Revelation 2:7, 11, 17, 29; 3:6, 13, 22). When the people of God can no longer hear Jesus, their rebellion is almost complete. Jesus once said, "My sheep hear my voice and I know them and they follow Me" (John 10:27). It is to be noted that knowing Jesus translates into hearing Jesus' voice. This constitutes the verifying factor that sets us apart as Jesus' children. But is this true of us? That is, is it our testimony, and if it is not what does this say about our claim to be His followers?

CHRIST'S INVITATION

Christ's invitation in all cases is to overcome! That is, hear, repent, and pray (Revelation 2:7; 2:11; 2:17). The recipe for spiritual health is neither complicated nor difficult;

we should employ it every day. Actually, then, an "overcomer" is a failure who gets it right. He or she acknowledges sin and repents. Restoration and blessing are always the result, and we should employ these simple truths every day!

CHRIST'S REWARD

His promise is equally straightforward and simple: Those who hear and respond to His voice will reign in righteousness with Him in the eternal world to come and will receive new names, be pillars in the house of God, partake of the Tree of Life, and with Him rule the nations with a "rod of iron." The heavenly vision is sure, and it will not fail. A glorious eternal future awaits those who faithfully follow Jesus.

CHAPTER FOUR

SPECIAL DEVOTION

The Believer and Rewards

Jesus' message to the seven churches of Asia brings into focus the question of Christians being judged, scrutinized, and rewarded for their faithful service to Christ while on earth. Paul also refers to this reality in his epistles by reminding his readers that at the consummation of the age, and by Jesus' second coming, we shall all be judged before we take up our station in the eternal Kingdom of God. For Paul then, we shall appear before the "bema" (judgment) seat of God, and our works will be truly scrutinized. The truth will be out for all to see, and we will have no place to hide! Happy will be the believer who hears the words, "Well done, good and faithful servant. . . . Enter into the joy of your Lord" (Matthew 25:23).

In 1 Corinthians 3:11–15, Paul reflects on this inescapable appointment before the throne of God and tells us that our works will be evaluated and placed in one of three categories. That is, they will be likened to gold and silver; precious stones; or wood, hay, and straw. Those whose works fall into the last category will enter Heaven but without reward. How sad this will be, because it will remain the situation for all eternity! It will thus be highly embarrassing to be an eternal rewardless Christian.

LIVING IN THE LIGHT OF ETERNAL JUDGMENT

This reality surely brings into focus the nature of our everyday activities, and even more, the attitudes and actions of the heart that initiate these activities. The future is truly the present, and we would do well to remember this and treat every day as if it were our last! It is worth stressing that from this passage we learn that this judgment of the believer will not decide whether he or she will enter Heaven or not. It is the judgment of the genuine believer, the person who has truly repented of his sins and has trusted fully in Jesus' work on the cross to save him. It is this person's subsequent dedication to Christ while on

earth that will be scrutinized and rewarded! We should live appropriately.

THE IMPORTANCE OF RIGHT RELATIONSHIPS

In Romans 14:1–14, Paul again addresses this subject, but this time in the context of believer/believer relationships. These will be scrutinized on that great day when we shall appear alone before God. His punch line is, "So then each one of us shall give an account of himself to God." How we deal with fellow believers is important because it reflects on how we deal with Jesus, since He lives in them. This should wake us all up! In 1 Corinthians, chapter 11, Paul also reminds us that if we celebrate the Lord's death at the "Communion Table" without giving due respect and care to our believer/believer relationships, we shall "drink judgment unto ourselves." The regular celebration of the Lord's saving work, as reflected at the Communion Table, should prepare us for a better review when, on that final day, we will all stand before Him! This is why we are told to do this "until He comes again." On that great day when we stand before Him, He will either weep over us or joyfully reward us. Which will it be?

THE GREAT WHITE THRONE JUDGMENT

This judgment of believers is not to be confused with the Great White Throne Judgment referred to in Revelation 20. This final judgment is reserved for the damned—that is, those who have rejected God's grace and love in Christ and will thus be fairly judged, found wanting, and convicted and consequently banished from the presence of God and cast into the lake of fire for all eternity. Without effective atonement for sin, they are without hope, separated from the grace of God and ensnared by their own rebellion against God.

THE DIGNITY OF THE LOCAL CHURCH

All of this also brings into focus the dignity of the local church. It is not merely a meeting place but a unique body infused with God's Holy Spirit and therefore transformed into a sacred temple. The fullness of Jesus fills this body by His Spirit, and those who make it up are a royal priesthood who offer up in it and through it sacrifices of praise and service. We would do well to remind ourselves of the awesome nature of the Church and thus to engage our fellow believers with much love and care. In dealing with them,

we deal with Jesus, especially the weakest amongst them, and therefore we should make it our aim—as much as it is possible—to be right with God and right with our fellow believers all the time. God is watching!

THE THINGS ETERNAL

CHAPTER FIVE

THE MESSAGE OF THE ETERNAL THRONE ROOM

Immediately I was in the Spirit; and behold, a throne set in heaven, and One sat on the throne.

Revelation 4:2

We have already noted in this volume that the Book of Revelation is about the unveiling of Jesus—spiritually to the Church and eventually physically to the world. The events described in Revelation are required precisely so that this unveiling can take place. They are not random or haphazard by character, nor are they orchestrated at will by the Devil. No, they are necessary to prepare the Church for Jesus' coming, to prepare the world for

judgment, and to demonstrate that God's judgment is righteous and holy and seen to be so!

These are undoubtedly catastrophic judgments. The world will totter and fall under them and, as a consequence, men's hearts will be gripped by great terror as they sweep over and consume the earth. They are already here and growing in intensity with each passing day just as birth pangs become more painful and frequent as a mother prepares to give birth. Days of great shaking are upon us, and of this we have been forewarned!

> *...but now He has promised, saying, "Yet once more I will shake not only the earth, but also heaven."*
>
> Hebrews 12:26

This being so, the Book of Revelation takes us to the splendor, stability, and settled authority of Heaven before it paints the awful and awesome picture of what is to shortly befall the earth. We are thus introduced to "things eternal." All in all, two scenes, both having to do with the Throne of God, are placed before us. The first scene is that of the Sovereignty of God and the second is of Christ's redemptive work. We need to hold both scenes dear and close if we want to survive the days that are surely approaching.

GOD'S SOVEREIGNTY—CHAPTER FOUR

"You are worthy, O lord, to receive glory and honor and power; for You created all things, and by Your will they exist and were created."

Revelation 4:11

Here John is introduced to God's throne, which is absolutely transcendent, far removed from all of creation, and "hangs in nothing." The scene unfolding before him is overwhelming and amazing. On a vast sea of glass sits a throne that is ablaze with light and glory the likes of which he has never seen. Arching over the throne is an Emerald Rainbow and from the throne itself, like spears of fire and light, comes a glory and presence that can only be attributed to the "One" who sits on it. The reality of this "One" fills everything, and before Him are seven burning lamps of the Holy Spirit and a Heavenly Court, or Sanhedrin, comprised of twenty-four Elders and four great Beasts or Living Creatures of differing likenesses. The Beasts resemble a Lion, a Man, a Calf, and an Eagle, and they all have six wings by which they move with great speed and everywhere. These all give glory to God; this they do day and

night, thus extolling the character of God and rejoicing in the fact that He created all things by the word of His great power. In short, He is the Creator of the universe!

This universe exists by Him and for Him and thus He controls it, maintains it, and will never give up on it! "The earth is the Lord's and the fullness thereof." The rebellion of the Devil, with a third of the heavenly host and the rebellion of humankind against God will not now or ever dethrone God! All will serve His eternal purpose, and in due time the earth will finally enter into the reason for which it was created. Even those who rebelled against Him will bow the knee and confess that He is God.

> *I have sworn by Myself; the word has gone out of my mouth in righteousness, and shall not return, that to Me every knee shall bow, every tongue shall take an oath. He shall say, "Surely in the LORD I have righteousness and strength. To Him men shall come, and all shall be ashamed who are incensed against Him."*
>
> Isaiah 45:23-24

THE LESSON

The lesson is sure: God is in control of His world, now and forever! This picture of a sovereign, all-powerful throne anchored John and gave him a foundation upon which to stand. We too must feast our eyes upon this incredible picture, for the days ahead will become so turbulent, confusing, and catastrophic that, if our eyes are not upon the Throne of God, we might waver, be deceived, and fall. Jesus has already warned that so terrifying will be the events unfolding on earth just before His coming a second time that even the elect could fall prey to deception (Matthew 24:24).

We must know and believe in our hearts that God is sovereign, in control, and doing what is right.

GOD'S REDEMPTION—CHAPTER FIVE

And they sang a new song, saying: "You are worthy to take the scroll, and to open its seals; for you were slain, and have redeemed us to God by your blood out of every tribe and tongue and people and nation, and have made us kings and priests to our God; and we shall reign on the earth."

Revelation 5:9-10

A perfect God made a perfect world for perfect human beings to live in. His work of creation has stages and is still underway, because the prize, or pinnacle, of this creative work of God is perfect men and women—perfect as in reflecting the image of God! Humankind's rebellion against God in the Garden of Eden did not therefore take God by surprise. It was just the first step toward an end that would produce a perfect being to live in a perfect creation. Man's ability to reason and make decisions had to be exercised and ultimately harnessed by the Creator. That is, men and women must choose to love and serve God because they now know that the alternative choice only brings forth misery and death. So Paul tells us that the whole of creation is longing and groaning for the day when it can spring back into its real beauty and perfection so as to greet the arrival of a "perfect landlord." This landlord is us!

> *For the earnest expectation of the creation eagerly waits for the revealing of the sons of God. For the creation was subjected to futility, not willingly, but because of Him who subjected it in hope; because the creation itself also will be delivered from the bondage of corruption into the glorious liberty of the children of God. For we know that the whole creation groans and labors with birth pangs together until now.*
>
> Romans 8:20-22

Thus the introduction of sin into the world was part of the process of creating a new creature. Adam, having drunk from the "well of death," with us all in him, now knows the bitterness of making wrong choices and of rebelling against God. The way of a perfect God is the only way, and we have only discovered this by tasting the "wormwood and gall"! The fall of humankind did not therefore lead to "plan B," as it was always part of one plan that is still unfolding before our eyes and that will come to its conclusion by the Revelation of Jesus. Indeed, the one and only plan of God required a redemptive initiative to bring forth the creature that God always wanted.

JOHN'S HOPELESSNESS

John, having been ushered into the very throne room of God, realizes that humankind's fall from the presence and character of God is so far that no one can breach the chasm and return Adam and Eve, and thus the whole human race, to the throne room—to the presence of God and to fellowship with God. He weeps! Reconciliation between God and humankind is an impossibility, since the very best of humankind's good works, even those of Mother Teresa, cannot breach this chasm and reconcile us to God. God's

righteous standard, as reflected in His Moral Law, is far too high. Our good works are at best dead works (Ephesians 2:8-9; Hebrews 6:1)!

Sin, rebellion against God's holy character as reflected in the Ten Commandments, has not only separated us from God, but it has also brought us under the wrath and curse of God. We have no way of rectifying this as the bar is too high. The Law, which is good and holy, has become our judge and convicts us and confirms us in our wickedness, sin, and hopelessness. This awful truth dawns on John, and he then realizes that the view he has seen of Heaven and God's glorious throne will never be enjoyed by a sinful and fallen world. No deliverer from our world or earthly king can redeem the fallen human race, and so the glory that he has just seen is a fading dream that will never become a reality for anyone on earth. The only just expectation for the human race is to be eternally banished from the presence of God and "deposited" in the dark realm of the living dead! John is wholly overcome with grief and weeps. This is how he puts it: "So I wept much, because no one was found worthy to open the scroll, or to look at it" (Revelation 5:4).

THE SEVEN-SEALED SCROLL

The seven-sealed scroll signifies the title deed to Heaven and Earth. The One who can pay the price to "buy humanity back" qualifies to open the seals and thus to take possession of all that God has created. This created order, including humankind and things in heaven and on earth (Ephesians 1:9-10) can be reconciled to God by the One who can pay the price. This One, as it turns out, could only be God Himself. But would He pay the awful price demanded by His character, given that His creatures, in need of reconciliation, have become His enemies and have trampled underfoot His likeness and thus deserve His wrath? How would He ever step down from His throne to do such a thing? Once again John sees no chance of this happening and weeps.

In actual fact the scroll imagery is not new; it reflects the legal cultural practices in Israel in that day and earlier. In Bible times, when one purchased a plot of land, one was given a seven-sealed scroll, which was a legal document giving title to the land in question. Even though you had paid for the land, it only became yours when you actually went to it, placed your feet on it, and broke the last, or seventh, seal. We see this reflected in the piece of land that Jeremiah

bought at Anathoth. He left the city of Jerusalem in a time of siege to take possession of his purchased land by breaking the seventh seal with his feet on the property. Those around him thought he was trying to flee, but in fact he was simply obeying the law in order to take possession of that which he had rightfully bought (Jeremiah 32).

THE LAMB

John's grief is relieved, because suddenly his eyes behold a Lamb, "as if slain," standing in front of the throne of God. This Lamb, full of purity, innocence, and meekness and fully divine, has stepped out of the eternity and the glory of Heaven into time, space, and matter and has paid the price, by the spilling of His own blood, for the redemption of the human race and all things in heaven and on earth. God has done for His world that which no one thought possible, and the thing that motivated Him to endure such pain and sorrow at every level is love! The heavenly court acknowledges this great act of sacrifice and rightly ascribes glory and honor to the Lamb.

> *Then I looked, and I heard the voice of many angels around the throne, the living creatures, and the elders; and the number of them was ten thousand times ten thousand, and thousands of thousands, saying with a loud voice: "Worthy is the Lamb who was slain to receive power and riches and wisdom, and strength and honor and glory and blessing!" And every creature which is in heaven and on the earth and under the earth and such as are in the sea, and all that are in them, I heard saying: "Blessing and honor and glory and power be to Him who sits on the throne and to the Lamb, forever and ever!" Then the four living creatures said, "Amen!" And the twenty-four elders fell down and worshipped Him who lives forever and ever.*
>
> Revelation 5:11-14

This Lamb was actually foreordained before the foundation of the world to undertake His holy redeeming work. That is, before God made anything the Son gave His word to His Father that He would come into the world, assume a human body and die for the sins of the human race. This remarkable truth is reflected in various passages of the Bible.

All who dwell on the earth will worship him, whose names have not been written in the Book of Life of the Lamb slain from the foundation of the world.

Revelation 13:8

Therefore do not be ashamed of the testimony of our Lord, nor of me His prisoner, but share with me in the sufferings for the Gospel according to the power of God, who has saved us and called us with a holy calling, not according to our works, but according to His own purpose and grace which was given to us in Christ before time began.

2 Timothy 1:8-9

Thus, in the long view of things, sin's entry into the world did not take God by surprise. Before time began, He knew that in order to acquire a heavenly family to live with Him eternally, He would have to let them first go into sin and rebellion. This would prove to them that the ways of God are to be desired, chosen, and loved. More than this, it would prove to them that God Himself is love and can be trusted with every part of our lives. Our time and pilgrimage on Earth would prepare us for eternal service and glory! No wonder the hosts of Heaven sang, "Worthy is the Lamb

who was slain to receive power and riches and wisdom and strength and honor and blessing."

THE TRUTH OF THE SEVEN-SEALED SCROLL

It is important to note, then, that the seven-sealed scroll contains the whole program by which God, by Jesus Christ, triumphs over the wickedness and evil of the world. The breaking of each seal describes the nature of end-time events, thus ultimately bringing us to the consummation of the age and the return of Jesus Christ to the Mount of Olives. When the last seal is opened, Jesus will put His feet on this holy mountain and take full and final possession of all that is in the world. He will rule the nations with "a rod of iron," nations will not "learn war anymore" and the "knowledge of the Lord will cover the earth as the waters cover the sea."

The judgments that follow, namely the Trumpet and Bowl judgments, in the main body of the Book of Revelation describe in greater detail the events unfolding by the breaking of the seven seals. They therefore do not run in sequence but in parallel! It is crucial to grasp this fact. Furthermore the Seal Judgments are similar in nature and sequence to the "signs of the times" that Jesus gave us in the

Synoptic Gospels of Matthew, Mark, and Luke. When one understands this, the next part of the Book of Revelation, which is Things Eschatological, becomes clear. God wants us to see the big picture, and then we can arm ourselves and prepare ourselves to face the dangerous and pressing challenges of the end-time.

Don't be fooled; the whole Book of Revelation is for the whole Church! There is one Second Coming of Jesus, and this is not in stages or phases as some assert. This Day, oh glorious Day, will take place at and just before the great Day of God's wrath, which is not the Great Tribulation. A time of great testing awaits the people of God, and I fear that a theology of escapism has left much of the Church ill-prepared and weak! More about this later.

THE LATE HOUR

Given the similarities between the Seal Judgments and the end-time signs that Jesus gave in Matthew 24, I am personally convinced that Jesus is already opening the Seals in Heaven, and we are presently observing the consequences of this on Earth. He is initiating the process that will witness Him taking full possession of that which He died for on the cross and rose again for on the third day. This

breaking of the Seals is leading to an intense—yes, very intense—eruption of tribulation and conflict on the Earth. The powers and systems of darkness are intensifying their struggle against the Church and Israel, and they will not easily give up. Indeed, even when facing utter and complete destruction and expulsion from the earth, by the revelation or coming of Jesus, they will unify their efforts and resources in an attempt to oppose the coming Son of God.

> *And I saw the beast, the kings of the earth, and their armies, gathered together to make war against Him who sat on the horse and against His army.*
>
> Revelation 19:19

No matter what, Jesus will triumph and His feet will stand on the Mount of Olives and He will eject the devil and his following hordes from the earth. The hour is late, the day draws nigh, and Jesus will be triumphant! Of this we can be sure.

CHAPTER SIX

SPECIAL DEVOTION

The Divinity of Jesus

The glorious picture presented to us in the segment of the Book of Revelation we have called Things Eternal introduces us to the subject of the divinity of Jesus. The Lamb before the throne is not simply empowered by His sacrificial death to open the sealed document, but He is supremely qualified to do so because He is God. Thus He is worshipped and adored, a practice reserved only for God Himself (Revelation 5:12, 13). It is His spotless and sinless life that enabled Him to lay His life down and take it up again (John 10:17-18). His indestructible life qualified Him to make atonement for the sins of the world. Concerning Jesus, Hebrews 7:16 states, "who has come, not according to the law of a fleshly commandment, but according to the power

of an endless life."

Only God can receive worship (Exodus 20:3-6), and thus the fifth chapter of the Book of Revelation clearly sets forth the fact of the divinity of Jesus! This truth is absolutely vital and important to understand, because today there are many in the so-called confessing church that are denying or casting doubt upon Jesus' divinity.

PLAYING ON WORDS

They assert with accuracy that the term Trinity does not appear in the Bible. This is true. However, the facts that demand the use of the term do. No one in two thousand years of Church history has come up with a better term by which to describe the nature of the Godhead as revealed on the pages of Scripture. Jesus is God! He is of the very same essence of God and even said it in John 10:30: "I and My Father are one."

The word in the Greek here means "one indivisible entity." He also took the name of God as it was revealed to Moses when He stated, "before Abraham was, I AM" (John 8:58). The Jews of His day clearly understood what He was asserting and took up stones to kill Him, because they believed His comment to be blasphemy and worthy of

death (John 8:59). In fact, it was precisely this claim to be God and equal with God in every way that ultimately sent Jesus to the cross for execution. His detractors were so sure that no man could claim to be God that they confidently accused Him of blasphemy, found Him guilty, and sentenced Him to death.

Then the high priest tore his clothes, saying, "He has spoken blasphemy! What further need do we have of witnesses? Look now you have heard His blasphemy! What do you think?" They answered and said, "He is deserving of death" (Matthew 26:65-66).

The truth is: He was and is God. It was precisely this perfection that made His life indestructible and therefore capable of dying and rising again from the dead so as to free us forever from the tyranny and awful consequences of sin. This was no play on words or game of bluff. His claim, as outrageous as it appeared to be, was true, and it sent Him to His death! Paul fully captured this wonderful truth when he penned these words to Titus:

> *For the grace of God that brings salvation has appeared to all men. Teaching us that denying ungodliness and worldly lusts, we should live soberly, righteously, and godly in the present age looking for the appearing of our*

> *great God and Savior Jesus Christ, who gave Himself for us, that He might redeem us from every lawless deed and purify for Himself His own special people, zealous for good works.*
>
> Titus 2:11-14

JESUS IN HIS OWN WORDS

It is important then to note that Jesus performed the following acts:

- Claimed pre-existence with God His Father before the universe ever came into being (John 17:5).

- Received worship, which is reserved for God alone (John 20:8; Revelation 5:13).

- Asserted that He was indeed God and equal to our Father in Heaven (John 14:7-11).

- Took the name of God as His own without hesitation (John 8:58).

The truth about Jesus' identity is thus clear and unambiguous. He claimed to be one with God, to be God, and to have existed with God before the world was ever created.

As the saying goes, "If it looks like a duck, speaks like a duck, and acts like a duck, then it must be a duck!" Jesus is God!

FURTHER BIBLICAL EVIDENCE

Numerous Old Testament passages in the Bible that refer to God the Father are attributed to Jesus in the New Testament. Here are two of them:

1 In Psalm 102:24–27, David addresses God:

I said, "O my God, do not take me away in the midst of my days; Your years are throughout all generations. Of old You laid the foundation of the earth, and the heavens are the work of Your hands. They will perish, but You will endure; yes, they will grow old like a garment; like a cloak You will change them, and they will be changed. But You are the same, and your years will have no end."

In the Book of Hebrews, the writer affirms that David was writing about Jesus (Hebrews 1:10-12).

2 In Isaiah chapter 6, the prophet sees a vision of the throne of God and thus of the glory of God. He describes it thus: "In the year that King Uzziah died, I saw the Lord on a throne, high and lifted up, and the train of His robe filled the temple."

In the twelfth chapter of John, the disciple declares that Isaiah actually saw Jesus and spoke of Him (John 12:37-41).

THE TESTIMONY OF THE LETTERS

The various letters written by Paul and John and the author of the Book of Hebrews clearly demonstrate that they all considered Jesus to be God: One with the Father and the Spirit from all eternity. Thus Paul, in the letter to the church at Philippi, writes that Jesus, "being in the form of God, did not consider it robbery to be equal with God" (Philippians 2:6). That is, Jesus was not taking anything from God when He claimed to be God. In his letter to the Colossians, he asserts that Jesus was the "instrument" of creation. That is, God the Father, in the power of the Holy Spirit, used Him to create all things. Paul writes, "He is the image of the invisible God, the first-born over all creation. For by Him all things were created that are in heaven and

that are on earth, visible and invisible, whether thrones or dominions or principalities or powers. All things were created through Him and for Him. And He is before all things, and in Him all things consist" (Colossians 1:15-17).

There is thus only one conclusion we can come to: Jesus is God!

The writer of the Book of Hebrews wraps it all up, as it were, when he states, speaking of Jesus, that God:

> *...has in these last days spoken to us by His Son, whom He has appointed heir of all things, through whom also He made the worlds; who being the brightness of His glory and the express image of His person, and upholding all things by the word of His power; when He had by Himself purged our sins, sat down at the right hand of the Majesty on High...*
>
> Hebrews 1:2-3

CONCLUDING THOUGHTS

John, the beloved apostle, tells us in his first epistle that the Word of life, that is eternal life, that was always one with the Father way back before time and creation ever began, has been manifested and thus seen, handled,

and witnessed to by the apostolic band. This is Jesus and therefore God Himself (1 John 1:1-4)! This is the One that lives in us by His Spirit, because we have repented of our sins, and based on what He did for us on the cross we have invited Him to be Lord of our lives. Jesus is truly the God-man. He was never created but begotten as He came into the world (John 1:14) for the sake of sinners. He is also perfect man and thus, as Revelation chapter 5 teaches, the only One qualified to die for our sins and thereby reconcile us to God.

To deny the divinity of Jesus is serious, because if you do, you cannot be saved. Understanding the Trinity is not easy, but it is necessary for one to be saved. Only God can save us, and He did! Isaiah writes, "I, even I, am the Lord, and besides Me there is no savior" (Isaiah 43:11). Truly, the Godhead is a mystery, and so it should be because if we understood it we would be God!

And without controversy, great is the mystery of godliness:

God was manifested in the flesh,
Justified in the Spirit,
Seen by angels,
Preached among the Gentiles,

Believed on in the world,

Received up in glory.

1 Timothy 3:16

THE THINGS ESCHATOLOGICAL

CHAPTER SEVEN

A SCROLL WITH SEVEN SEALS

Now I saw when the Lamb opened one of the seals; and I heard one of the four living creatures saying with a voice like thunder, "Come and see."

Revelation 6:1

Eschatology is the study of the "last things," that is, the things that have to do with the consummation of the age. The main body of the Book of Revelation deals with these matters. It is an amazing resource and should be studied very carefully, though few in the Church do. Unfortunately, those who neglect its study will be impoverished spiritually and robbed of a blessing! "Blessed is he who reads and those who hear the words of the prophecy, and keep those things which are written in it; for

the time is near" (Revelation 1:3).

Chapter 6 introduces us to the actual breaking of the seals on the scroll that appeared with Jesus at the throne of God. As we noted, the scroll is the title deed to all that is in Heaven and on Earth. It was purchased with the blood of the Lamb. Of note is the fact that the content of the Seven Seals approximates to the signs of the times that Jesus gave us in Matthew 24. This is no coincidence; it is a "heavenly pattern" enabling us to better understand the Word of God. Both passages address the following issues in exactly the same sequence:

1. **The coming of false Christs**
   Revelation 6:1 / Matthew 24:4–5

2. **Wars and rumors of war**
   Revelation 6:3–4 / Matthew 24:6

3. **Disputes between nations on a global scale**
   Revelation 6:5–6 / Matthew 24:7a

4. **Famines, pestilence, and natural disasters**
   Revelation 6:7–8 / Matthew 24:7b

5 **Persecution of Christ's followers**
Revelation 6:9–11 / Matthew 24:9–14

6 **The sign of the coming of the Son of Man**
Revelation 6:12–17 / Matthew 24:29

7 **The triumph of the purpose of God**
Revelation 8:1–5 / Matthew 24:30–31

It is to be noted that between the opening of the sixth and seventh seal there is a parenthesis in which a picture is given of the saints of all ages who now appear before the throne of God. They have come out of the Great Tribulation, and therefore they are the victorious family of God! Matthew 24 has the same parenthesis wherein it warns about the coming Great Tribulation (see Matthew 24:15-28).

This great company of the redeemed is from every nation and tribe. They include Israel, and they have all been saved by the blood of the Lamb. They are so huge in number that they cannot be counted. John describes this amazing scene like this:

After these things I looked, and behold, a great

> *multitude which no one could number, of all nations, tribes, peoples, and tongues, standing before the throne and before the Lamb clothed with white robes, with palm branches in their hands...*
>
> Revelation 7:9

When asked where they came from, John wisely says, "Sir, you know." The answer given by one of the elders is this:

> *These are the ones who come out of the great tribulation, and washed their robes and made them white in the blood of the Lamb. Therefore they are before the throne of God, and serve Him day and night in His temple. And He who sits on the throne will dwell among them.*
>
> Revelation 7:14-15

A SPECIAL PEOPLE

This great multitude that no man can count is a special people. Their walk with Jesus was pure and true, and they are rewarded by being given a unique place near to the throne of God. The "Olive Tree" of Romans 11 has finally attained "resurrection of the dead" as a consequence of the

people of Israel having been "grafted" back into their own spiritual tree (Romans 11:12-26). In other words, there will be no resurrection or life from the dead for the Church until the people of Israel are restored spiritually. There are not two "fullnesses of the Gentiles" in the Bible! Many teach that after the fullness of the Gentiles have been gathered into the special family of God, they will be "raptured" (taken out of the world by Christ) and then Israel will be saved and evangelize the world. That is, another "fullness of the Gentiles" will be gathered in! The Bible does not teach this anywhere, and Paul clearly says that when the fullness of the Gentiles has been gathered in and saved, then Israel will be saved by a coming deliverer (Romans 11:25-26). I say again, there are not two "fullnesses of the Gentiles" in Scripture.

Moreover the passage teaches us that at the end of the Great Tribulation, just before the Day of the Lord, the Day of His great wrath, the Church is taken out of the world, "raptured," and greets Christ as He comes a second time, in great glory and power and in flaming fire to judge the world of the ungodly! About this fact the Bible is absolutely clear. That is, the first and only day that Christians still living on Earth will see Jesus for the first time is on the same day that He descends from Heaven to judge the Earth.

This is what Paul affirms in 2 Thessalonians 1:6-10. This passage is clear, unambiguous, and simple to understand. Furthermore, it is not contradicted by any other part of Scripture.

THE GREAT TRIBULATION

It is therefore important for us to note that the Great Tribulation is merely the climax to a path of tribulation that the faithful people of God have walked through the ages. John introduces the Book of Revelation to us in chapter one by declaring that he is a brother in Christ and thus a "companion in the tribulation and kingdom and patience of Jesus Christ" (Revelation 1:9).

In all ages and at all times, the Church of the living God has had to face Great Tribulation. The early Christians were butchered by Rome, and just in the last decade two million Sudanese Christians were murdered by Islamic radicals in South Sudan, now the Republic of South Sudan. Many had their limbs cut off and were impaled on trees and left to die. What could be worse? But the lazy, fat, sleepy western Church wants an escape route to avoid all trouble at all costs.

The final Great Tribulation is so named because it will

be the greatest trial for believers in that it will be global in nature. Hitherto these trials have been regional, but all of this is about to change. You should be warned, prepared, ready, and dedicated to Jesus, who said that Christians would be hated by all nations before He comes again (Matthew 24:9). An unprecedented persecution is coming to the body of Christ. Many of God's servants have warned of this, including the late David Wilkerson. Indeed, even as I write, the Church everywhere in the West is being driven out of the main street and from society. Recently teachers in the United States were accused of committing a crime because they bowed their heads in reverence while others prayed in a public place! The day of thought crimes has arrived!

THE TRUTH WE SHOULD KNOW

Scripture is clear that the Great Tribulation is not the Day of the Lord nor the Day of His Wrath! If this be true, then there is no reason why Christians should not have to go through and face the Great Tribulation. So the book of Matthew affirms that immediately after the Great Tribulation the "sun will be darkened and the moon will not give its light" (Matthew 24:29). By contrast, the book of Acts

states that the "sun will be darkened and not give its light" before the great and terrible Day of the Lord will arrive (Acts 2:20). So clearly, the Day of the Lord—the Day of His wrath—is separated from the Great Tribulation by the changing of the luminaries. This settles the argument once and for all and should make Christians rethink their escapist theology.

According to Paul and to the Book of Revelation, as the luminaries change after the Great Tribulation and the Day of the Lord begins to break in upon the earth, the Church, living and dead, is resurrected to meet the Lord as He comes in the air (1 Thessalonians 4:13-18). This, as we have already noted, harmonizes completely with his teaching in 2 Thessalonians 1:6-10. This too was the teaching of the early Church, and it can be supported from the remaining documents of this period. In terms of Jesus' coming for His Church, the Bible does not teach a "secret rapture." The so-called pre-tribulation rapture teaching is an invention of the nineteenth century that was never taught in the Church before.

THE REAL ISSUE

The real issue is not that of suffering, tribulation, and death but of dedication to Jesus. If we have surrendered our lives totally to Him and made Him Lord of all that we are, then this matter has been dealt with. We lay down our lives for Him in whatever way He desires because He is Lord of our lives! Christians eaten up with fear in this regard contradict the work of God in their lives because "He has not given us a spirit of fear, but of power and of love and of a sound mind" (2 Timothy 1:9). If we are filled with fear, then we have a real spiritual problem and there is something wrong with our commitment to Christ. When He reigns in our lives His love casts out all fear (1 John 4:18).

Paul knew that he was facing a cruel death, but he had no fear. The same was true of Peter; in fact, Jesus forewarned him that he would die as a martyr (John 21:18). This meant, according to Jesus' own words, that he would be crucified. Peter had to live with this notion for the rest of his life, but he did so with grace and dignity and even wrote about it in his second epistle. (2 Peter 1:12-15). He was not afraid and counted it a joy to suffer for His Lord. Why should this not be true of us?

THE DAYS IN WHICH WE LIVE

The Seven-Sealed Scroll constitutes the big picture of end-time events, just as Matthew 24 does. It alone appears before the throne of God, since it is the title deed to Heaven and Earth purchased by the blood of the Lamb. When its seventh seal is broken, Jesus takes possession of all that He has redeemed by His death. The other judgments flow out of this scroll, not in sequence but in parallel. They give the micro and more detailed picture of the big picture. They even describe, as we shall see, the same events. However, the Scroll Judgments warn us of much of what we see on the earth today. We could go on and on describing in boring detail the nature of the calamities, at every level, that beset the world today. You know of them. Wars and rumors of war abound, as do natural, financial, and medical problems. Earthquakes strike every side of our globe, and Israel is back in her ancient homeland. Jesus said that when we see all these things taken together, including the restoration of the Jews to Jerusalem, then know that the end is nigh. You should now know this (Mark 13:29)! Look up, because your redemption is drawing nigh!

CHAPTER EIGHT

SPECIAL DEVOTION

The Fellowship of His Sufferings

For many Christians, the pathway of tribulation and suffering is to be rejected. It is nowadays not uncommon to hear preachers who, by cleverly stringing together a systematic theology, support this notion. It plays well with human carnality. Quite simply, however, they are wrong! A biblical theology will prove otherwise, as does the history of the Church. For centuries God has required of His people to walk through the valley of suffering and pain. The Book of Revelation warns of this reality. Its writer, John the Apostle, was imprisoned on the Island of Patmos when he wrote it, having received it from Jesus. Also, in His message to the church of Smyrna, Jesus warns that the devil is about to cast some of His dear followers into great tribulation. His only

comforting word to them is, "be faithful unto death!"

> *Do not fear any of those things which you are about to suffer. Indeed, the devil is about to throw some of you into prison, that you may be tested, and you will have tribulation ten days. Be faithful until death, and I will give you the crown of life.*
>
> Revelation 2:10

It is to be noted that this is one of only two churches that escape rebuke from Him. They are a faithful and dedicated church, like that at Philadelphia, and yet they are to be tested by suffering! In this word "tested" we have the reason for, or answer to, our trials and sufferings as God's children.

THE WAY OF THE CROSS

Jesus said that we are to pick up our cross daily and follow Him (Luke 9:23). This means, by the life of Christ within us, we are to overcome our sinful nature. Our trials, troubles, and sufferings are redemptive because they further this holy work. Peter writes in his first epistle, "He that hath suffered has ceased from sin" (1 Peter 4:1). In fact, in the same verse he says that as Jesus suffered so you should

arm yourself with the same mind. That is, as a Christian, expect suffering! We should note the following, then:

- Suffering comes to us by the will of God (1 Peter 3:17).
- Suffering refines our character to approximate more fully to that of Christ's image (1 Peter 4:1).
- Suffering enables us to reach people for Jesus who otherwise would not be reached (Philippians 1:12-13).
- Suffering encourages the people of God to better serve Christ (Philippians 1:14).
- Suffering enables us to compassionately comfort those who are also passing through various trials and troubles (2 Corinthians 1:3-7).

Paul urges us in the Book of Philippians to enter into the fellowship of Christ's sufferings, for it is only by traveling this road that we will truly get to know Him (Philippians 3:10). This is not to say that we look for suffering or even desire it, but rather to know that when it comes, and it will, we will embrace it with a godly perspective and trust in Christ. By it we are trained, corrected, and purified. We must see this as a privilege, for again, Paul writes:

For you it has been granted on behalf of Christ, not only to believe in Him, but also to suffer for His sake...

Philippians 1:29

The writer of the Book of Hebrews addresses a suffering church and calls upon the church members to get some backbone and endure, since God is correcting them as a father would his children, and indeed, if they are without this correction and discipline they are not really His Children. These are strong words indeed—truly words that should be addressed to much of the Church today (Hebrews 12:3-11). In the end, our trials bring our characters to a place where they reflect Jesus in a lost and dark world. Our lives become redemptive, and they shine like a lighthouse showing the way. James knew this and wrote the following words:

My brethren, count it all joy when you fall into various trials, knowing that the testing of your faith produces patience. But let patience have its perfect work, that you may be perfect and complete, lacking nothing.

James 1:2-3

Peter concedes that sometimes the day of trial and suffering comes upon us as something strange and

unfathomable (1 Peter 4:12-13). However, as we remain faithful, it too will pass, and even if it doesn't it will bring us great reward. Paul's life was a never-ending cycle of suffering, yet he saw the redemptive benefits built into his many trials, persecutions, and disasters. They were laying up for him "an eternal weight of glory" (2 Corinthians 4:16-18). You need to examine all these Scriptures carefully and then "arm yourself," as Peter writes, or recognize, as the writer of the Book of Hebrews does, that God our Father faithfully leads all His children by this way. It is unavoidable!

It is finally worth noting that we do not have to understand everything that happens to us as Christians. There comes a time in our walk with God that He expects us to trust Him even though we cannot see the purpose behind our troubles. At this time you need to remain convinced that He is doing the right thing for your life and will ultimately settle you down and bring you to a place of rest. Happy is the Christian who has been trained by this process.

> *But may the God of all grace, who called us to eternal glory by Christ Jesus, after you have suffered a while, perfect, establish, strengthen, and settle you.*
>
> 1 Peter 5:10

CHAPTER NINE

THE TRUMPET AND BOWL JUDGMENTS

But in the days of the sounding of the seventh angel, when he is about to sound, the mystery of God would be finished, as He declared to His servants the prophets.

Revelation 10:7

Behold, I am coming as a thief. Blessed is he, who watches, and keeps his garments, lest he walk naked and they see His shame.

Revelation 16:15

While the breaking of the Seven-Sealed title deed to heaven and earth is the "big picture" relating to Things Eschatological,

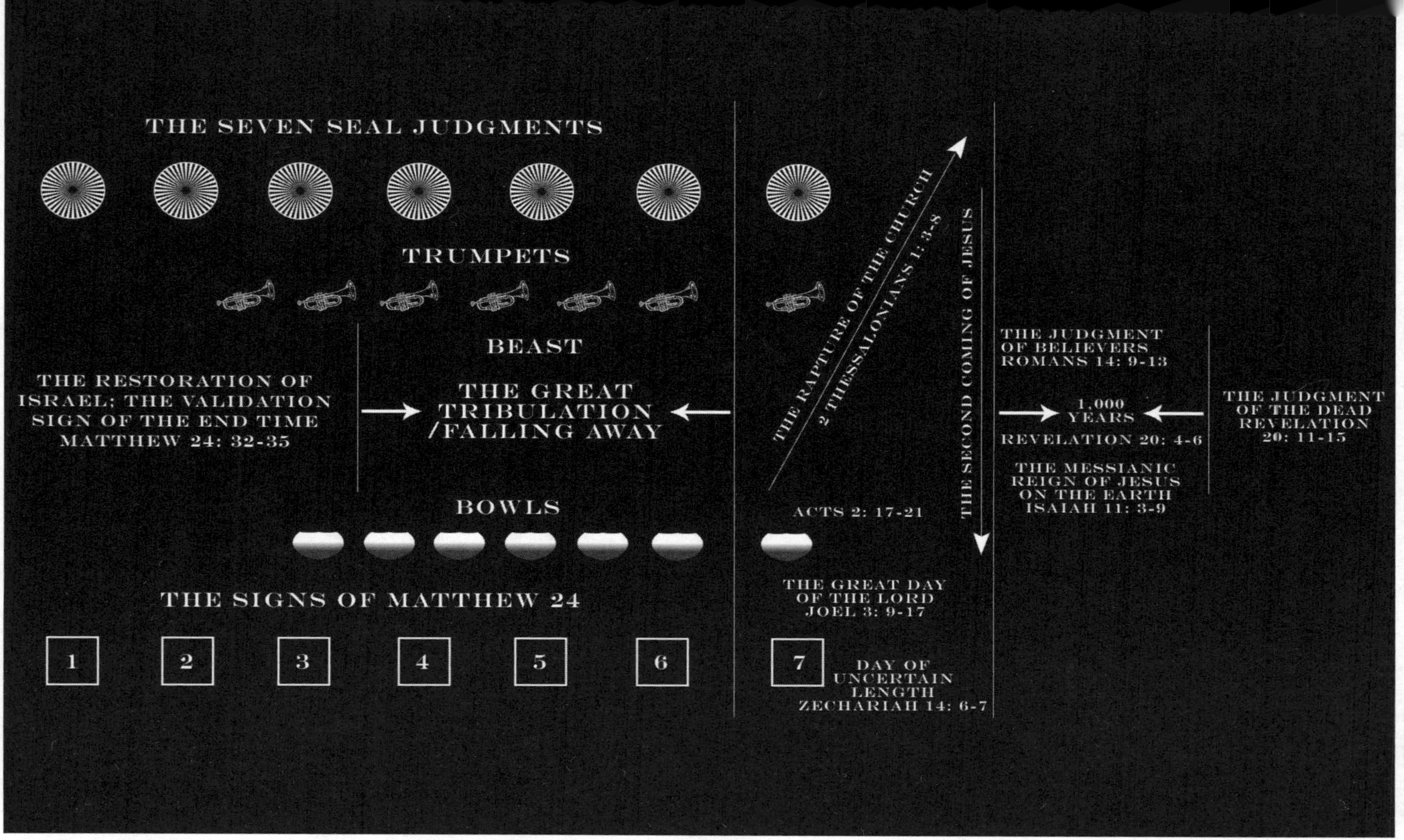
THE SEVEN SEAL JUDGMENTS
TRUMPETS
BEAST
THE RESTORATION OF ISRAEL; THE VALIDATION SIGN OF THE END TIME MATTHEW 24: 32-35
THE GREAT TRIBULATION /FALLING AWAY
BOWLS
THE SIGNS OF MATTHEW 24
1
2
3
4
5
6
7
THE RAPTURE OF THE CHURCH
2 THESSALONIANS 1: 3-8
ACTS 2: 17-21
THE GREAT DAY OF THE LORD JOEL 3: 9-17
DAY OF UNCERTAIN LENGTH ZECHARIAH 14: 6-7
THE SECOND COMING OF JESUS
THE JUDGMENT OF BELIEVERS ROMANS 14: 9-13
1,000 YEARS
REVELATION 20: 4-6
THE MESSIANIC REIGN OF JESUS ON THE EARTH ISAIAH 11: 3-9
THE JUDGMENT OF THE DEAD REVELATION 20: 11-15

the Trumpet and Bowl judgments constitute a more detailed description of end-time events. They fill in the gaps and they too are not to be seen as being in sequence but in parallel. The diagram on the opposite page will help you understand this.

It is to be noted that, while they are staggered in parallel, that is, they describe great cataclysmic and natural upheavals in the Earth, they eventually harmonize—the sixth Trumpet and the sixth Bowl judgments picture the same events as does the seventh in both cases. In both instances a great army from the East crosses over the River Euphrates and encircles Israel. This is the "preparation event" for the Day of Armageddon or the great Day of the Lord; the Day of His wrath!

Then the sixth angel sounded: And I heard a voice from the four horns of the golden altar which is before God, saying to the sixth angel who had the trumpet, "Release the four angels who are bound at the great river Euphrates." So the four angels, who had been prepared for the hour and day and month and year, were released to kill a third of mankind.

Revelation 10:13-15

> *Then the sixth angel poured out his bowl on the great river Euphrates, and its water was dried up, so that the way of the kings from the east might be prepared. And I saw three unclean spirits like frogs coming out of the mouth of the dragon, out of the mouth of the beast, and out of the mouth of the false prophet. For they are spirits of demons, performing signs, which go out to the kings of the earth and of the whole world, to gather them to the battle of that great day of God Almighty.*
>
> Revelation 16:12-14

It is thus important to note that this also harmonizes with Matthew 24 and the breaking of the sixth and seventh Seals. Also, in all cases there is a parenthesis between the sixth and the seventh Seal judgments, as we have already noted, and between the sixth and seventh Trumpet judgments and the sixth and seventh Bowl judgments. This is the place of the Rapture or the removing of the Church from the Earth—after the Great Tribulation but before the Great Day of God's Wrath! So at the Last Trumpet, the "mystery of God" on the Earth is finished or brought to a conclusion (Revelation 10:7) and just before the seventh Bowl Judgment, when the nations are being readied for Armageddon, Jesus prepares to come like a thief (Revelation 16:15), an analogy that Paul used in 1 Thessalonians 5:1-6.

It can't get clearer than this! Jesus' second coming, like a thief, is at the end of the Great Tribulation and before the day of God's wrath. No wonder Paul writes that we should be watchful and sober. It was, after all, Paul who also wrote that the Church is removed from the Earth at the blowing of the Last Trumpet (1 Corinthians 15:52; 1 Thessalonians 4:13-18). With this the Book of Revelation agrees and most certainly does not contradict the rest of Scripture. The last trumpet is indeed the last trumpet, and when it is blown the rapture will take place.

Moreover, the "mystery of God" in Scripture is the Church (Ephesians 2:8-13; Romans 16:25-27). At the blowing of the Last Trumpet, this mystery finds its conclusion on the Earth. Awesome days lie ahead, and we must ensure that we are prepared and ready; yet I fear that too many Christians are sleeping and looking for an escape route that will deliver them from trial and tribulation.

UNDERSTANDING THE BOOK OF REVELATION

It is also important to note that the harmonization of these judgments contradicts any notion that these judgments are in sequence, or one after the other. They are not, and further proof of this is that at the blowing of the

Seventh Trumpet the consummation of the age comes and Jesus begins to rule and reign over the nations.

> *Then the seventh angel sounded: And there were loud voices in Heaven, saying, "The Kingdoms of this world have become the Kingdoms of our Lord and of His Christ, and He shall reign forever and ever."*
>
> Revelation 11:15

Likewise, at the outpouring of the Sixth Bowl judgment and going into the seventh, the great Day of Armageddon is upon the Earth (Revelation 16:12-16). The Book of Revelation, since it is written by a Jew, is written in the classic form, or structure, of Hebrew parallelism. That is, similar concepts are laid side by side, giving us an alternative view of the same thoughts or pictures.

PAY ATTENTION

It is also important to note that these judgments deserve close scrutiny and attention because they give us a warning of what the "shakings of God" will look like. To be forewarned is to be armed and delivered from all fear. There will be great conflicts and upheavals in the Earth in the near future, such as have not been seen before (Matthew

24:21). The seas and rivers will be polluted, earthquakes will shake continents, wars will exact a heavy and gruesome toll on human life, fish and animal life will disappear and become extinct, and a global government and world financial system that hates everything that Jesus stands for will arise, bringing persecution to the people of God. All of this is in the Book of Revelation, and much of it is happening now! Are you ready and prepared?

When you know that God, not the devil, is shaking the world in this way, then you have no fear (Hebrews 12:25-29). These shakings are designed to undermine every false foundation upon which humankind stands, and by so doing bring it to repentance. They are ultimately manifestations of God's love as it is the only way that He can get the attention of a rebellious and lost world. Hell was never made for men and women but only for the devil and his angels (Matthew 25:41). Our Lord will do anything to steer people away from it!

Sadly, the rebellion and wickedness of the human heart is such that it will not repent and return to God, even though Jesus provided a once and for all sacrifice on the cross for the sins of the world (Revelation 16:11). The "broad way" will lead to eternal destruction, and many are they who travel this road (Matthew 7:13).

CHAPTER TEN

SPECIAL DEVOTION

A Time to be Honest

For too long, the wider Christian Church in the West has tolerated a teaching on the Second Coming of Jesus that enjoys no biblical basis. This sounds incredible, but it is in fact true. By this I mean the so-called pre-tribulation rapture teaching. It has taken root in the Western Church because it suits the comfort and ease of its existence and because it tells Christians that they will not suffer any tribulation but rather be raptured away from it before it begins! This is a nice theory, and even I wish it were true, but then again I look at hundreds of thousands of South Sudanese Christians who were martyred for their faith in Jesus over the last two decades and were thus brutally murdered.

In fact, the Book of Revelation reveals that believers in the Great Tribulation will suffer a similar fate, but certainly not as

gruesome, as their martyrdom will be swift and clinical—they will be beheaded (Revelation 20:4)!

The theological reason said to be behind this pre-tribulation rapture theory is the notion that the Great Tribulation of the end time is a manifestation of God's wrath and, since Christians have been delivered from God's wrath by the death of Jesus, they will be spared it. Are these facts true? No, they are not! The idea that the Great Tribulation is the Great Day of the Lord or the Day of His wrath is not true. According to Scripture, in fact, the Great Day of the Lord or the Day of His wrath takes place after the Great Tribulation. Thus there is no reason why Christians should not have to endure this period. They have endured times like this of old and they will again.

So let's be clear about a few things:

1 We all believe in a rapture and thus we all own the events spoken of in 1 Thessalonians 4:13-17. This chapter by no means validates a pre-tribulation rapture position. It does, in fact, apply to a funeral service, and it simply notes what will happen when sleeping (dead) saints are called forth from the grave by the Second Coming of Jesus. Again, nowhere does it describe a position that endorses a

pre-tribulation rapture theory.

2 According to Matthew 24:29 and Acts 2:20-21, the luminaries are changed after the Great Tribulation but before the Day of the Lord. So the awesome and terrible Day of the Lord is not the period known as the Great Tribulation! This totally undoes the pre-tribulation rapture thesis.

3 According to 2 Thessalonians 1, the only and first time that believers will get rest from their struggles and trials on earth is when Jesus comes in "flaming fire" on the Day of The Lord to judge and damn the ungodly. That is, believers will be raptured and caught up to meet Jesus, not at some secret coming but on the very day when He comes in great glory and flaming fire to judge the world and take control of it! The context of this passage is more than clear about this and cannot be denied. (Note verses 6-10.)

4 According to Paul in 2 Thessalonians 2, the Day of The Lord is the same Day as that of Jesus' coming again. He actually states that we should

not be deceived about Jesus' coming as this will not happen until two things occur: a great apostasy and the rise of the Son of Perdition or Antichrist (verses 1-3). These, according to Paul, are the final two signs that believers are to look for in order to avoid deception and be assured of Jesus' imminent coming. He even goes so far as to say that they must remember that when He was with them He told them these things (verse 5). Why would he warn them about these things if they were simply not true because they would be raptured beforehand? To teach that the restraining influence of verses 6 and 7 is the Church or Holy Spirit is just conjecture—actually, if it is one of these, this would be a violation of the context. It would make nonsense of the passage! It would be like saying, "I will meet you next week for lunch," when I know all along that I am leaving today for three weeks in London. The fact is, the only restraining influence in the Bible is an angelic one. Angels are positioned at key points in time restraining the advance of evil, as they did at Sodom and Gomorrah, in Daniel's great visions, and as they do now at "great pressure points" of the world. When the Lord God of Heaven calls upon them to leave, they will release

a surge of evil upon the world and with it judgment (Revelation 9:13-15; Genesis 19:12-16). This view is true to the context and to the rest of Scripture. Again I say: the only restraining influence in all of Scripture is that of Angels!

5 Jesus told His Disciples to expect to go through the Great Tribulation (Matthew 24:15). This verse not only warns the founders of the Church that they will have to face the coming Abomination of Desolation, but it is also edited by Matthew to warn all those who ever read it. The final Abomination of Desolation is yet to come (2 Thessalonians 2:4-5), and we would do well to take heed. As Paul writes, "Remember that when I was with you I told you these things." The Book of Revelation not only speaks of suffering saints living under an Antichrist reign, but it also praises them for their endurance and promises them a unique dwelling place in Heaven (Revelation 7:13-17; 13:10; 14:12-13). According to pre-tribulation rapture pundits, these are mostly backslidden saints who were left behind at the rapture. I think not.

6 None of the Olivet discourses in the Synoptic Gospels speak of a secret rapture, even though Jesus was speaking to His Disciples and therefore to the Church. They only portray one Second Coming of Jesus, in glory and majesty like lightning flashing from the East to the West, and He urges all His followers to watch and pray about this coming day. I once debated a pre-tribulation rapturist and referred the audience to this fact as my opening statement, and the expert consequently jumped up and stated that Jesus allowed His Disciples to believe this because He knew that Paul would come later and rectify it! My question was, "What else has Jesus lied about?" The truth is, the Second Coming of Jesus is not in two phases but simply one. It is the Second Coming and not the third coming. We, according to Scripture, look for this day (Hebrews 9:28).

7 There is a sound historical argument against the pre-tribulation rapture teaching: if one reads the documents of the early church for the first three centuries and more, one will find it nowhere mentioned. Only the visible Second Coming is mentioned with anticipation and excitement. In fact, this

teaching is nowhere mentioned by any of the great biblical expositors of history. Not one. It was first taught in the early 1800s and originated in a meeting of the Closed Brethren in Scotland in 1830. A woman called Margaret MacDonald gave a prophetic utterance in one of their meetings that was construed as a "new revelation" on the Second Coming. This utterance was codified, and eventually people like Derby and Irwin began to aggressively propagate it. It gained rapid acceptance because it promised an escape from suffering and, indeed, none of us want to suffer—not even me! Still, it is a false teaching.

8 The most troubling aspect of pre-tribulation rapture teaching is that it undermines the once for all finished work of Jesus on the cross! Pre-tribulation rapture proponents believe that the Church and Holy Spirit are removed from the Earth before the seven-year period of Great Tribulation. As a consequence, they teach that so-called tribulation saints are saved by returning to the Law, or by Jesus, but without the gift of the Holy Spirit, etc. This is just nonsense—it undermines the once for all death of Jesus on the cross; because of this death, the Old

Covenant with its animal sacrificial system has forever been abolished (Hebrews 9:9-10; 8:13). There will be no return to it. Moreover, the poured-out gift of the Holy Spirit is part of what Jesus purchased on the cross (Acts 2:29-33; John 7:37-38). To teach that the Holy Spirit is removed from the Earth even though people still get saved is an attack against the atonement of Christ.

9 The pre-tribulation rapture teaching is also a denial of the nature and character of the Church. According to Paul, Gentiles, with less ease than Jews (Romans 11:24), are grafted into a Jewish spiritual tree called an Olive Tree (Romans 11:17-18). They are then advised not to be arrogant or boastful toward the fallen Jewish branches that because of unbelief in Jesus are not in the tree (Romans 11:18). These will at some point be grafted back into their own tree. When this happens, the whole tree will be resurrected or raptured (Romans 11:12, 15). Paul's reasoning is clear: if a negative in Israel (their rejection of Jesus) brought a positive for the Gentiles (saved and grafted into a Jewish spiritual tree), what will happen when a positive

takes place in Israel (acceptance of Jesus' messianic credentials)? The answer he gives is, "resurrection from the dead!" Thus, any theory of the rapture that leaves Israel to suffer and die alone while the Church is whisked away to Heaven is not biblical. This is precisely what the pre-tribulation rapture teaching does. The rapture takes place when Israel is grafted back into her own tree, not before!

And, just for the sake of clarity, there are not two "fullnesses" of the Gentiles in Scripture. Paul declares that when the "fullness of the Gentiles" is saved then "all Israel will be saved" (Romans 11:25-26). That's it! Pre-tribulation rapture teachers would have us believe that there is a first fullness of the Gentiles, then a rapture, and then another fullness of the Gentiles brought about by saved Jews who evangelize the world. This is not biblical! When Israel is "grafted back" into her own spiritual tree, Jesus comes again, a second time, and reigns from Zion (Romans 11:25-26).

There is much more that one could write about this matter and, in closing, it is worth noting that Paul, when writing to the Thessalonians, told them that Jesus is not

coming as a thief for the Church, because the Church will definitely know the season of His return (1 Thessalonians 5:1-6). Jesus' second coming catches the ungodly as a thief in the night. It is surely time to be honest about this, warn the Church as we see the Day approaching and prepare for all that is coming. If I am wrong, I have only strengthened the Church, but if I am right, then much of the Western Church has been deceived and will be caught off guard! Who will sound the alarm?

CHAPTER ELEVEN

THE GREAT SIGN CHAPTERS

Now a great sign appeared in heaven: a woman clothed with the sun, with the moon under her feet, and on her head a garland of twelve stars.

Revelation 12:1

THE ZOOMING EFFECT

When one watches a major sporting event, the cameras covering the fast-moving pace of the game on the field will, from time to time, zoom in on the key and well known players, thereby bringing them into closer focus on the screen. In this way, one can see them more clearly and understand the positions they

occupy on the team more fully. The same principle applies to the Book of Revelation. There are some key players who will dominate end-time events on Earth. It is for this reason that the book draws our attention to them in the hope that we will identify them and prepare accordingly. There are four in all:

1. **The Two Prophets**
   Revelation 11

2. **The Nation of Israel**
   Revelation 12

3. **The False Christ**
   Revelation 13

4. **Babylon**
   Revelation 17-18

THE TWO PROPHETS

Revelation 11 introduces us to two people who appear in Jerusalem in the Temple Compound. They are unique in that they have very powerful ministries that attract global hatred and resistance. They prophesy, meaning forth-tell or preach, at the altar of sacrifice. This firstly means that at some point in the near future, the Temple that once stood on Mount Moriah will be rebuilt. God alone knows how this will happen, but be assured it will! Secondly, they enjoy a unique calling and purpose. The whole world will be impacted by their ministry, and even the natural elements will be affected as they strike the earth at will with plagues and judgments.

> *These have power to shut heaven, so that no rain falls in the days of their prophecy; and they have power over waters to turn them to blood, and to strike the earth with all plagues, as often as they desire.*
>
> Revelation 11:6

As a consequence, they are hated and eventually martyred, and shortly thereafter they rise from the dead and ascend into heaven. The question is, "Who are these men

and what purpose, under God, do they serve?"

A STARTLING TRUTH

The clues to their identity are found in the passage. According to the text, they are the "two olive trees" that stand before the Lord of the whole earth (Revelation 11:4). This statement is what Jewish expositors of the Bible call the principle of remez. That is, this one-line statement is intended to "drive" one to the passage of the Bible where this matter is more fully written about—in this case, the fourth chapter of the Book of Zechariah. By referring to this larger section of text on the matter, one will come to an understanding of its meaning. Peter employed this method of exposition on the day of Pentecost when he quoted from the Book of Joel. He said, "This is that . . ." (Acts 2:16). In other words the principle of remez means that if you want to know more about this, then see that! So, let's do precisely that.

ZECHARIAH 4

This chapter is about the rebuilding of the Temple in Zechariah's day and beyond. He is called a restoration

prophet because he helped to encourage the exiles, who had returned from Babylon/Media-Persia to Jerusalem after the seventy-year exile that began in 586 BC to complete the building of the Temple. The Prophet Haggai fulfilled a similar role. However, having set this context, the fact that the Book of Revelation foresees a future scenario like that of Zechariah's day makes chapter 11 of Revelation very fascinating and interesting. The Book of Revelation was written by John the Apostle sometime around 92 AD. Jerusalem and the Temple had been destroyed by the Romans in 70 AD, and yet John sees a "new" Temple on Mt. Moriah that will be built, thereby setting the context for Zechariah 4 to be fulfilled again! It is all about restoration! The end-time Temple will serve a very significant purpose, and the Two Prophets are central to this. Events then and now in Jerusalem were and are so chaotic and challenging that it is hard to believe that a Temple will rise again. It is totally outside of the realm of human possibility. Thus we have one of the most famous verses in all of the Bible, given to us in Zechariah's fourth chapter:

> *"Not by might nor by power, but by My Spirit," says the LORD of hosts.*
>
> Zechariah 4:6

In other words, the Spirit of God will accomplish this work of restoration, and this begs the question, "Why is the rebuilding of the Temple so important to the Spirit of God?" The short answer is, "Because it will result in the Spirit of the living God being poured out over the people of Israel." Wow!

THE DETAILED PICTURE

Zechariah sees two olive trees standing before the Lord of the whole earth. They impart olive oil, a symbol of the Holy Spirit, to a Menorah, the symbol of Israel, and thereby light it up. In short, Israel will again be ablaze with the power and light of the Holy Spirit of God. All this is achieved by the rebuilding of the Temple. What happened in Zechariah's day will happen again just before Jesus comes again and after the Jews have been restored to Zion after a long exile of two thousand years. These days are upon us!

In other words, Israel is spiritually restored and renewed by the ministry of the "two olive trees," who according to Revelation 11 are Two Prophets. By the miraculous hand of God, the Temple will be rebuilt on the Temple Mount east of the Old City and west of the Mount of Olives. This Temple will not be built next to the Mosques presently

standing there. This is the "theory of unbelief" and is only held by those who do not believe in the power of God's Spirit. These Mosques will come down, and a third Temple will arise on the sacred mountain. Just watch and see!

MOSES AND ELIJAH

The Two Prophets are easily identified based on the principle of remez as the only Prophets who had power to bring down plagues on the earth and who were able to control the elements: Moses and Elijah. Revelation 11 clearly states that this will be their mode of operation, with worldwide consequences (Revelation 11:5-6). No wonder they will be hated from one end of the Earth to the other. It is also worth noting that both these men are the revered fathers of Israel. Elijah is considered the great prophet of Israel, and at the end of his ministry, he was taken up into heaven in a chariot of fire (2 Kings 2:11). He therefore never died, even though "it is appointed unto men once to die . . ." (Hebrews 9:27). He brought fire down from heaven and shut up the heavens so that it could not rain (1 Kings 17:1).

Moses, on the other hand, is famous for the plagues that he brought down upon Egypt (Exodus 10-11), but he

also died in very strange circumstances: his body was also taken into heaven by the Archangel Michael, who disputed with the Devil over it (Jude 9). In other words, his body was not allowed to decompose, indicating that God had a special use for it that the Devil wanted to prevent.

Still more amazing is the fact that both of these men appeared alive, in human bodies, with Jesus on the Mount of Transfiguration (Mark 9:1-6). The question then has to be asked: "What type of bodies did they have, given that Jesus had a human body?" They most certainly did not have glorified bodies, because Jesus is the first fruits of the resurrection (1 Corinthians 15:20-23). That is, He is the first human being to emerge from the grave in a glorified body! Moses and Elijah appeared with Jesus on the holy mountain, giving witness to His messianic credentials. And since Jesus had not yet died and risen from the dead, they all had human bodies. Moses, representing the law, and Elijah, representing the prophets, bore testimony to Jesus' identity and soon coming passion (Luke 9:30-31). The prophet Malachi tells us that before the great and terrible Day of The Lord, God will send Moses and Elijah to unite the family of God (Malachi 4:4-6)—that is, to unite the fathers to the children. This is a clear reference to a work of restoration that will bring Israel (the father) together with the Church (the

children). This, of course, is exactly what Paul teaches in Romans 11. Israel's spiritual recovery will unite it with the Church and will result in resurrection from the dead (Romans 11:15). Without a family to rule with Christ over the earth, God will curse the earth (Malachi 4:6)! Thanks be to God; He has brought forth just such a family and they will rule and reign with Christ over the nations (Revelation 2:26-27).

A REMARKABLE MINISTRY AND CALLING

Moses and Elijah, being the great spiritual fathers of Israel and representing the accepted canon of the Hebrew Scriptures, will come again at the very end of the age to point Israel to Jesus by prophesying at the altar in the Temple, which is a picture or symbol of the cross. Israel has always claimed that Moses and the Prophets (Elijah) do not speak of Jesus and His death. Jesus Himself contradicted this theory as, when walking with His forlorn disciples on the road to Emmaus, He, "beginning with Moses and all the prophets, explained to them in all the scriptures the things concerning Himself" (Luke 24:27). He also, in the days of His ministry, told a story about a rich man and a poor man called Lazarus (see Luke 16). The rich man

died and went straight to hell because of his wickedness. Lazarus, though poor, was a godly man, and when he died he went to paradise, or Abraham's Bosom. Overcome with eternal anguish and suffering, the rich man demanded of Abraham that Lazarus should be sent back to Earth to warn his family and friends about the horrors that awaited them if they did not repent and change their ways. Abraham refused, saying, "They have Moses and the Prophets (Elijah); let them hear them."

In other words, Israel needs to hear Moses and Elijah! God, in His great love and mercy for Israel, has kept them waiting in heaven and will send them back to "restore all things." This is why Jesus stated that Elijah will yet come and restore all things (Mark 9:12). Moses and Elijah will appear in the Temple, at the altar of sacrifice, and preach on the cross by using the altar as a visual illustration of what Jesus did at Calvary (Revelation 11:1-6). By the power of the Holy Spirit, they will bring salvation and restoration to Israel, the Menorah of God. This is precisely why the Temple has to be rebuilt: not to reintroduce an obsolete system of animal sacrifice but to serve as a visual illustration of the once for all finished work of Jesus on the cross. This is what the writer of the Book of Hebrews does as he addresses faltering believers, and this is precisely what

happened when Jesus died. The Veil in the Temple was split from top to bottom (Luke 22:45), symbolizing that the way into the very presence of God had now been opened by Jesus' death (Hebrews 9:6-12). A third Temple will shortly rise on Mount Moriah in Jerusalem, and when it does, the stage will be set for one of the most dramatic encounters that will ever be witnessed on that site. It will happen, "'not by might nor by power, but by My Spirit,' says the LORD" (Zechariah 4:6).

SETTING THE RECORD STRAIGHT

Israel's unbelief or blindness has been a topic of much discussion and debate. The question must be asked, "When and how did this take place?" Certainly Israel's unbelief did not commence with her rejection of Jesus' messianic credentials, even though this is the standard or regular view on this matter.

Actually His own "received Him not" because of something pertaining to Moses that took place 3300 years ago. Moses was responsible for Israel's blindness! Moses witnessed, and was visibly touched by, the glory of God when he climbed up Mt. Sinai to receive from God the Ten Commandments engraved, by the very hand of God,

on two tablets of stone. He then descended to his people, waiting at the foot of the mountain, with the Law in his hands and with his face shining with the glory of God. The message, at first, was clear and for all to see: the way back to God and His glory is through the keeping of the Law. Sadly, Moses failed to let the Israelites see that in reality the glory of God upon his countenance was diminishing. He thus covered his face so that the departing glory could not be observed by Israel; by so doing, he left them with the false notion that the way back to the glory of God and character of God is by keeping the Law. From that day forward, Israel believed the lie, blindness covered their hearts, and any other notion of salvation would be rejected. This remains true to this very day!

> *Therefore, since we have such hope, we use great boldness of speech–unlike Moses, who put a veil over his face so that the children of Israel could not look steadily at the end of what was passing away. But their minds were blinded. For until this day the same veil remains unlifted in the reading of the Old Testament, because the veil is taken away in Christ. But even to this day, when Moses is read, a veil lies on their heart.*
>
> 2 Corinthians 4:12-15

The truth was, the Law reveals the high standard of God's character that no person can reach. "All have sinned and fall short of the glory of God" (Romans 3:23). This is the truth that Moses should have allowed his people to see and understand when he lived among them after coming down from the holy mountain. Sadly he did not, so he will have to come back and set the record straight. Thus he will appear with Elijah once again, and together they will give testimony at the altar to the finished work of Jesus on the cross. When He lives in us, we are truly filled with the hope of glory.

ENOCH AND JOHN THE BAPTIST

Some assert that Enoch may be one of the Two Prophets of the end time because he too was taken up into heaven without ever dying physically (Genesis 5:24). This is true, but he had no relevance to Israel or the Jewish people, because he was a pre-diluvian. Rather he is a type of saint who walks with God and who will be taken away, by death or resurrection, to be with Him forever. Christians don't die, they just sleep, but they are with the Lord. Being saved is one thing but we must all remember that the grace of God in Jesus calls us to a life of holiness "without which we

shall not see the Lord" (Hebrews 12:14).

John the Baptist was not Elijah. He came to Israel in the "power and spirit of Elijah" (Luke 1:17) but he did not fulfill the final calling over Elijah's life to be the restorer of Israel. Jesus acknowledged that John partially fulfilled Elijah's calling by becoming a forerunner, but He went on to affirm that Elijah would still be coming and was scheduled to return to finish the job (Mark 9:11-13)—that is, to prepare Zion for the Second Coming of the Lord.

THE NATION OF ISRAEL

Once again, the camera zooms in on the key player on the end-time field of play: the nation of Israel. The whole of chapter 12 is dedicated to the call, place, role, and destiny of this people. We should take careful note of its teaching, as it will give us the strength to fight the "good fight of faith" and the knowledge to understand the nature and plans of our adversary.

THE RULES OF IDENTIFICATION

Here once more the principle of remez applies, as the first great sign that appears before John's eyes is that of a

woman clothed with the sun, the moon, and twelve stars.

> *Now a great sign appeared in heaven: a woman clothed with the sun, with the moon under her feet, and on her head a garland of twelve stars. Then being with child, she cried out in labor and in pain to give birth.*
>
> Revelation 12:1-2

While expositors have literally "run wild" with this imagery, the truth is that this is a quote from the book of Genesis. The principle of remez teaches us that "this is that"; therefore the "that" in this instance is found in chapter 37 of Genesis. Here Joseph has a vision of his father and mother, the sun and the moon, and of his eleven brothers who, with himself, make up twelve stars (Genesis 37:9-11). Thus the truth is unmistakable; the woman of Revelation 12 is Israel, not the church!

THE ROLE OF THE WOMAN

The woman that John sees is pregnant. This is precisely the role that Israel has played out, through the centuries, on behalf of the world. She constitutes God's birthing people and, as such, is the vehicle of world redemption. This is a one-of-a kind calling, and it was precisely this call that

God laid upon Abraham when He called him forth from Ur of the Chaldeans. God said to Abraham, "In you all the families of the earth will be blessed" (Genesis 12:1-3). Israel births God's purpose into the world. Another way of putting it is to say, "Israel exists for the world, and she was called forth supernaturally in order to amplify God's voice to it." Jesus acknowledged this call over Israel when He said, "Salvation is of the Jews" (John 4:22). However, Israel exists for Jesus! While she has given us God's Word (Romans 3:1) and God's great men and Covenants, she has chiefly given us Jesus (Romans 9: 1-5). John sees her pregnant with a male child. Jesus is the great gift of Israel to a lost and dying world. She birthed a Godman into the world who, by His atoning death on the cross, has abolished death and brought eternal life to those who will repent and believe on Him (Titus 3: 3-7). The Male Child she brings forth is destined "to rule the nations with a rod of iron" (Revelation 12:5).

THE WOMAN'S ADVERSARY

The one great sign of the woman is followed by another: that of a red Dragon who has seven heads and who opposes the woman seeking to destroy her and her Child.

And another sign appeared in heaven: behold, a great, fiery red dragon having seven heads and ten horns, and seven diadems on his heads. His tail drew a third of the stars of heaven and threw them to the earth. And the dragon stood before the woman who was ready to give birth, to devour her Child as soon as it was born. She bore a male Child who was to rule all nations with a rod of iron. And her Child was caught up to God and His throne.

Revelation 12:3-5

As I have just stated, Israel exists for Jesus! She was pregnant with Him, and her destiny is to bring Him into the world twice! Once to die for the sins of the world, and once to return in glory and splendor to reign over it. He will be an absolute—but perfect and loving—Dictator. This Jesus buried in "the womb of Israel" was destined to, and did, destroy the works of the Devil in the world. He did this through the cross!

Having disarmed principalities and powers, He made a public spectacle of them, triumphing over them in it [the cross].

Colossians 2:15

Israel thus became the archenemy of the Dragon and will remain so. Having failed to destroy her at Jesus' first coming, he has now gathered all his forces, sadly even human ones just like the Nazis, in another attempt to annihilate her and thereby, as he sees it, to frustrate His soon return to earth. He knows that, according to God's word, Israel, by a process of restoration in her ancient homeland, will birth Him back into the world. His second appearing will finally eject the Dragon from the world, and thus a contest of huge proportions is mounting in the Middle East today. Through the centuries, the Dragon has used successive Gentile empires to attempt to destroy Israel; hence the seven-headed monster that John saw. He has failed, but even so, great suffering and sorrow has come to the Jewish people because of it.

Now with Israel's remarkable return to Jerusalem, the greatest conflict of all time is being set up by the Dragon. It has its origin in the heavenlies where great unseen powers are locked in battle with visible consequences on earth. John saw this too, as did Daniel, and they wrote of it in these terms:

> *And war broke out in heaven: Michael and his angels fought with the dragon; and the dragon and his angels*

fought, but they did not prevail, nor was a place found for them in heaven any longer. So the great dragon was cast out, that serpent of old, called the Devil and Satan, who deceives the whole world; he was cast to the earth, and his angels with him.

Revelation 12:7-9

At that time Michael shall stand up, the great prince who stands watch over the sons of your people; and there shall be a time of trouble, such as never was since there was a nation, even to that time.

Daniel 12:1

The Dragon is determined, one last time, to attempt to annihilate six million Jews who have returned from a two-thousand-year-old exile to settle again in the land of Canaan, promised to them by God as an everlasting possession (Genesis 17:7-8). He knows that the physical and spiritual recovery of Israel, unfolding in Zion today, will culminate with the Male Child returning to the Mount of Olives to rule the nations with a rod of iron. He must stop this process of the "restoration of all things," and thus he is mobilizing the whole world against Israel (Revelation 16:12-16). He will fail because God Himself watches over

Israel, and He will protect her in the "wilderness" of Canaan (Revelation 12:5-6).

To be sure, a huge conflict is upon us, and it is time for the people of God to wake up from their spiritual slumber before it is too late. Not only are we to "work while it is still day" by proclaiming the Gospel to the nations, but we should and must get into the spiritual battle on behalf of Israel. We share in "their spiritual things" (Romans 15:27), and are indebted to them, but more than this, we need to understand the significance of Israel's modern-day return to Canaan and Jerusalem. She is God's birthing instrument and has gone home, just as Jesus predicted (Luke 21:24), to birth the greatest event in human history: the return of Jesus to the Mount of Olives! The Church cannot and should not be disconnected from this final great event of history. She does so to her spiritual impoverishment!

A GREAT DECLARATION

The great conflict that erupts in the unseen but very real world is one-sided, because Michael and his angels overwhelmingly defeat the Dragon and his fallen angels. They are cast out of the second heaven from where they have ruled and influenced vast regions of the earth. Having

been dislodged, they descend to the earth to wage war one last time. That is, they will seek to annihilate Israel and destroy the Church of the living God, and they have one final "ace" to play (Revelation 12:9, 13-17). However, the Dragon's defeat is inevitable, and those redeemed by the grace of God have played a part in his defeat. They have worked with God, through prayer and intercession and works of righteousness, to secure a wonderful victory, but ultimately this victory has been theirs because of a great truth:

> *And they overcame him by the blood of the Lamb and by the word of their testimony, and they did not love their lives to death.*
>
> Revelation 12:11

They overcame because the grace of God, given in Jesus' death on the cross, reconciled them to God and, in the midst of a wicked generation, they held fast to their testimony and abandoned their lives to Jesus. True Christ followers live for Christ and, because of their commitment to Him, no longer live for themselves. This is what it means to embrace the name Christian. Anything short of committing fully to Jesus' lordship will not do and will not see us triumph over wickedness and overcome the evil of the end

time. These are issues that we should have resolved when we first gave our hearts to Jesus. Paul put it this way:

> *...and He died for all that those who live should live no longer for themselves, but for Him who died for them and rose again.*
>
> Corinthians 5:15

And Jesus said it this way:

> *"But why do you call Me 'Lord, Lord,' and not do the things which I say?"*
>
> Luke 6:46

This declaration of triumph is one that asserts the blessings won for us on the cross. We have no righteousness of our own, and by ourselves, apart from the grace and mercy of God, we can never be in a place of right standing with God. Our sins have condemned us to be banished from His presence forever (2 Thessalonians 1:8-9). The Dragon has reminded God of this time and time again (Revelation 12:10-11). He has accused us before the very throne of God, but God's love and mercy has covered our sins and we are perfect in His sight. We are free from the accusations of the Dragon and enslaved to the love and life of Jesus. Paul

always wrote that he was a "bond-servant" of Christ Jesus (Romans 1:1). This is how we should see ourselves.

THE FINAL ASSAULT

The Dragon, deprived of his aerial advantage, is cast down to the earth and recognizes that he now has only a short time. He is enraged and sets out to further his destructive campaign against Israel and the Church (Revelation 12:17). This will lead to the unveiling of his final weapon against the purpose of God. It is regrettable that chapter 12 of Revelation is disconnected from chapter 13 by this chapter division, as the one flows into the other. In other words, chapter 13 is the final assault that the Dragon launches in his diabolical plan to destroy Israel and the Church. This is his ace!

THE FALSE CHRIST

Our cameras sweep across the field and focus on another key player on the end-time field of play: the False Christ, Antichrist, or Beast. Scripture also refers to him as the Son of Perdition (2 Thessalonians 2:3). Here, and in the subsequent chapters, he is referred to as the Beast. He is the

final weapon that the Dragon has in his attempt to frustrate the will and plan of God for the world. This is a formidable weapon, and we should not in any way underestimate it. It will devastate the Church, as it will cause a great falling away, and it will deceive and enslave Israel and almost bring her to total destruction. These days are upon us! In fact the spirit of Antichrist is everywhere and getting stronger with each passing day (1 John 4:3). The Beast or False Christ is spoken of in many passages of scripture, including the three synoptic Gospels. This is therefore not an isolated teaching, and we would do well to take note of this. The Bible wants us to be prepared, and we will have no excuse if we are not, because much information is given about him.

THE CHARACTER OF THE BEAST

The beginning of chapter 13 refers us back to the Book of Daniel so that we can better understand what we are dealing with. In Daniel 7 we learn that the coming Beast Kingdom will have in itself the strength and wickedness of all the great empires of Daniel's time and beyond. It will thus have the combined strength and evil of the Babylonian (Lion), Media-Persian (Bear), Grecian (Leopard), and Roman empires (Daniel 7:1-7). It will thus be a formidable

kingdom that will embrace the whole Earth. Men will marvel at its scope and power and say, "Who is like the Beast? Who is able to make war with him?" (Revelation 13:4).

The power base of the Beast Kingdom will be a ten-nation confederacy of some type, and its spiritual DNA will be that of blasphemy!

> *Then I stood on the sand of the sea. And I saw a beast rising up out of the sea, having seven heads and ten horns, and on his horns ten crowns, and on his heads a blasphemous name. Now the beast that I saw was like a Leopard, his feet like the feet of a Bear and his mouth like the mouth of a Lion. The Dragon gave him his power, his throne, and great authority.*
>
> Revelation 13:1-2

The Beast Kingdom will belittle the God of Israel and our Lord Jesus Christ and aggressively pursue a global policy of persecution against those who follow Him. This will be no picnic!

THE ORIGINS OF THE BEAST

The Beast, according to Scripture, is a demonoid: he is and will be half devil and half man. He is therefore not

demon possessed but rather an incarnation of the devil or dragon. This is his ace! Scripture affirms that he comes up out of the "pit" or abyss (Revelation 11:7; 17:8). There is certainly mystery in all of this, but Jesus warned us that "as it was in the days of Noah, so it will be also in the days of the Son of Man" (Luke 17:26). The great evil of Noah's day was that fallen angels came down to the Earth and had sexual intercourse with women, thereby producing a demonic race (Genesis 6:1-3). In other words, demonoids have been here before! Thus, to save the human race from pollution and corruption, God sent a flood to destroy the demonoids, but he saved Noah and his family. Sounds too fantastic for words but it's all true, and it's about to happen again—only this time with greater wickedness and evil!

THE MISSION OF THE BEAST

The Beast will set out to destroy Israel by deception and to destroy the Church by false doctrine verified by signs and wonders. This is blasphemy! His incredible signs and wonders will seduce many, but those who know and hold the truth dear will stand firm and resist him (2 Thessalonians 2:11-12). He will seek to entrap the whole world spiritually by introducing a global religion linked to a global

financial system (Revelation 13:16-18). The mystery of iniquity (2 Thessalonians 2:7) is working in the world today as we witness it plunge toward global government and a one-world financial system. The chaos in our world financial markets will be rectified by a new international financial order. Governments everywhere are calling for this, and even the Vatican has made overtures in this regard. It's all just a matter of time, however. Lurking behind it all is a desire to sweep all traditional and historic religions aside in order to unify the world by demanding allegiance to a new religion, the object of which will be the worship of a demonoid! This is the bottom line and Revelation 13 warns of it.

> *Then he opened his mouth in blasphemy against God, to blaspheme His name, His tabernacle, and those who dwell in heaven. It was granted to him to make war with the saints and to overcome them. And authority was given him over every tribe, tongue and nation. All who dwell on the earth will worship him whose names have not been written in the Book of Life of the Lamb slain from the foundation of the world.*
>
> Revelation 13:6-8

The so-called Middle East Conflict between Israel,

her neighbors, and the Palestinians is without resolution. Politicians of all types and abilities, including the United Nations, the European Union, and the United States of America, have tried to resolve this conflict; but to no avail. It has remained a festering sore on the global political landscape, and it threatens the stability of the world. The Jews are themselves tired of war that, without end, feeds their children to the conflict. We would feel the same way. The Beast will solve this problem and thereby do what others have failed to do. Israel will welcome him—even more so because they will be able to rebuild their temple on Mount Moriah. The world will herald him as their true Messiah (2 Thessalonians 2:3-4). Deception and blasphemy will cover the earth and even Israel; but all of this will be permitted by the sovereignty of God! Why would God do this? In order to judge the world, purify the Church, and reveal Jesus to Israel. The "ace" that the devil will serve up for global consumption and control will be used to further the strategic plan of God. This is why Scripture affirms that God "has put it into their hearts to fulfill His purpose, to be of one mind, and to give their kingdom to the beast, until the words of God are fulfilled" (Revelation 17:17). Also, Paul writes that the delusions of Antichrist will be unleashed on the world by God Himself (2 Thessalonians 2:11-12). The

world is not spinning out of control, but it will receive its King and this King must and will come to Zion.

> *He who sits in the heavens shall laugh; the Lord shall hold them in derision. Then He shall speak to them in His wrath, and address them in His deep displeasure; "Yet I have set my King on my holy hill of Zion."*
>
> Psalm 2:4-6

This all has to do with setting the stage for the unveiling, or revelation, of Christ. Jesus' enemies must come to His footstool, and then He will rise up and crush them by His judgment, and thus, because they have all come out into the open for all to see, His judgment will be just and will be seen to be just.

> *But this Man, after He had offered one sacrifice for sins forever, sat down at the right hand of God, from that time waiting till His enemies are made His footstool.*
>
> Hebrews 10:12-13

Today Jesus' enemies are being made His footstool, and we have to discern and endure this process. It will be a very difficult period for the Church, but He will give us grace and power to be faithful just as He did to His first-century

followers. His word to us is found in this very chapter that warns of such evil things:

> *He who leads into captivity shall go into captivity; he who kills with the sword must be killed with the sword. Here is the patience and the faith of the saints.*
>
> Revelation 13:10

THE BEAST'S BROTHER IN ARMS

According to Scripture, the Beast comes up out of the sea, a reference to the nations and peoples of the world. However, his "brother in arms," the second Beast or False Prophet, comes up from the Earth (Revelation 13:11-12). He has "two horns like a lamb" and speaks "like a dragon," meaning that he is externally the epitome of innocence but is in fact empowered by the Devil himself. In other words he enforces the great deception produced by the Beast. Why would he come up out of the Earth? Because the second beast comes from a known region of the world! Daniel, once again, helps us to pinpoint the region of the second beast's origin in chapter 8 of his Book.

Here Daniel sees a Ram and a Goat locked in conflict.

The Ram is the Media-Persian Empire that is destroyed by the Goat, the Grecian Empire (Daniel 8:20-21). From the ashes of the Grecian Empire arise four "notable ones" (Daniel 8:8). One of these is a beast or antichrist (the second Beast of Revelation 13), and he gains great prominence in the region, even in "the Glorious Land," which is Israel (Daniel 8:9). He then commits great blasphemy, likens himself to God, and defiles a newly built Temple in Jerusalem on behalf of the first Beast (Daniel 8:11-12). He is truly a brother in arms!

While it is certain that this passage, in the first instance, applies to that which Antiochus Epiphanes did in 168 BC, it was referred to by Jesus as something that would happen again in the future (Matthew 24:15). It did, as in 70 AD Titus destroyed Jerusalem and desecrated the Temple. However, as with Jesus, Paul saw an end-time reoccurrence of this event by a "son of perdition" who would repeat the blasphemy and be destroyed, not by human hands but by the visible second coming of Jesus: "And then the lawless one will be revealed, whom the Lord will consume with the breath of His mouth and destroy with the brightness of His coming" (2 Thessalonians 2:8). Daniel 8 confirms that this is indeed also an end-time prophecy: "Understand, son of man, that the vision refers to the time of the end" (Daniel

8:17).

John, in the great nineteenth chapter of the Book of Revelation, which paints a magnificent picture of Jesus' second coming, also sees the "two beasts" of Revelation 13 apprehended by Jesus and cast into hell.

> *Then the beast was captured, and with him the false prophet who worked signs in his presence, by which he deceived those who received the mark of the beast and those who worshipped his image. These two were cast alive into the lake of fire burning with brimstone.*
>
> Revelation 19:20

So the point is clear—the false prophet or second beast will arise out of the Middle East region. I am personally convinced that the second beast of Revelation 13 has something to do with Islam. We must be watchful and prayerful, as the way all of this will work out is yet to be seen, but the Special Devotion at the end of this section will shed greater insight and light upon this matter. But one thing is sure: the Beast or Antichrist is supported by a second Beast, who enforces worship of the first Beast and enforces upon the world a new financial order that can only be accessed by the receiving of a mark on the hand or forehead (Revelation

13:15-18). No one will escape his net, and those who do and are found out will be put to death (Revelation 13:15)! This is not new, as it happened in Daniel's time (Daniel 3:8-12; 6:7-9) and again in the first and second centuries after Christ. Caesar-worship was introduced by the Roman Empire as a way to control the population, and those who would not confess that Caesar was Lord were put to death. The courageous story of Polycarp, Bishop of Smyrna and a disciple of John the Apostle, is from this period. He was burned at the stake because he cried out, "Jesus is Lord!" What will we cry out or are we asleep and ready to be ensnared by a "two-horned lamb."

One doesn't have to be a rocket scientist to see that a new world financial system is in the making. The chaos in our markets and crippling debt across the world is driving the international community toward a new financial order. Even the Vatican recently put out a statement calling for a new global financial system. Coupled with this is the growth of Islam and its infiltration into western societies—to such a degree now that vast regions of the once-Christian world are driving Jesus from the main street. Moreover, a commitment to political correctness everywhere is essentially banning the public preaching of the Gospel. This is the spirit of antichrist at work, and it will only increase

in intensity and influence. A recent proposal put forward at the United Nations will make it illegal, henceforth, for anyone to criticize Islam. A beast is arising out of the Middle East, and we must wake up, clean up, and stand up for Jesus!

THE IDENTITY OF THE BEAST

No issue has occupied prophetic scholars more than this one, and yet scripture itself tells us what to look for! In Revelation 17 the basic identity of the Beast is given in that he is one of seven kings presiding over an empire that is one of seven. The fact that he is apprehended and destroyed by the second coming of Christ means that he is the final empire or the seventh. John acknowledges this when he writes that five have already fallen, one is falling, that is the sixth, and then there will be the seventh. We can therefore forget the five that have fallen, the one that is falling is Rome, the sixth, and then there will be the Beast kingdom, the seventh. However, the Beast kingdom, though only one of seven, is also the eighth. This means that he comes twice and is thus seven and eight!

This passage affirms that the Beast of Revelation 13 comes twice as it states that the whole world will marvel

when they "see the beast that was, and is not, and yet is" (Revelation 17:8). It also confirms that when he comes as one of the seven he will at first "continue a short time" (Revelation 17:10). He will return as the eighth, and the whole world will marvel because they thought that he was dead, having received a mortal wound to the head (Revelation 13:3, 12; 17:8). Bearing in mind that the hatred and anger of the Beast and his brother in arms is directed toward Israel and the Church (Revelation 12:16-17), the Beast is someone who has been here before, for a short time, and has unleashed a vicious program of extermination against the Jews. It must also be someone who died from a head wound and who is well known to the generation living in the days of Israel's restoration. I believe that the beast could be (notice I said "could be") Adolf Hitler. His empire existed for only thirteen years, and yet he brought the world to destruction and murdered six million Jews. The point is, he has been here before, and thus our options in identifying him are narrowed down. Pray about it!

CHAPTER TWELVE

SPECIAL DEVOTION

The Forgotten Beast

Most end-time commentators give considerable attention to the Beast or Antichrist in their review of "last thing" events. However, the Bible warns that two Beasts will arise on the earth in the end time to challenge the purpose of God and His people, including Israel. The second Beast is called a False Prophet by scripture and is written about in the very chapter in the Book of Revelation that introduces us to the first Beast, or Antichrist: chapter 13 (Revelation 13:11-18). This tendency to concentrate on the Antichrist has blinded us to the dangers lurking in the Islamic world at this time. According to Scripture, this second Beast arises out of this part of the world. Both of these Beasts are finally apprehended and destroyed by Jesus' second coming

(Revelation 19:19-20; 2 Thessalonians 2:8). So we can safely conclude that the rise of a "two-beast" empire awaits us in the future! Let's look more closely at this matter.

CHRIST

An Apostle was sent from Heaven (John 6:37-40) into the world to die, the "just for the unjust," for the sins of the world (1 Peter 3:18). His death was a unique atonement, once for all, to reconcile us to God and thereby to also transform us internally (Titus 3:4-7; John 3:3).

ANTICHRIST

The Antichrist is an evil "beast" who has been here before (Revelation 17:8) and who arises out of the abyss to take control of a chaotic world with a political platform that approximates to that of ancient Rome (Daniel 2). Daniel sees four great world empires that dominate human history: Babylon, Media/Persia, Greece, and Rome. The Roman Empire has longevity in that it breaks in two, becomes two legs, and then, at the end of days, becomes ten toes. The same picture exactly is given of the Beast Empire in Revelation 13:1. It is this Beast and his empire that Jesus

destroys by His coming.

This Beast arises and enters the stage of history when the world is in economic and conflict-ridden turmoil, and Israel is back on the stage of history with Jerusalem as her capital (Luke 21:24). He will proclaim the arrival of a "new world order" and of a tolerant global religious system that will be a contradiction of Jesus' Gospel and be opposed to it (Revelation 13:1-10).

The Beast will be an enemy of the "blood-washed" Church of Jesus and will seek to eradicate it (Revelation 13:10; 14:11-12).

THE FALSE PROPHET

This is a "new Seleucid" king, arising out of the Middle East region, who will forge an alliance with the Antichrist kingdom that reigns over the world from Europe. It is the second and forgotten beast of Revelation 13. This Beast will honor a jihad, or god of war (Daniel 11:36-39), and those who oppose his rule will be beheaded (Revelation 20:4). It is to be noted that it is this Beast that finally invades Israel and commits the Abomination of Desolation in the Temple in Jerusalem (Daniel 11:36; 2 Thessalonians 2:4).

It is this Beast that enforces the rule of Antichrist and places the whole world under a new economic system that requires one to give religious allegiance to it in order to be part of it (Revelation 13:11-18). Beast worship will go hand in hand with economic activity. Hitler did the same thing!

One particular chapter of the Bible gives us a clear understanding of the rise and origins of the second Beast: Daniel 8. It tells us that Alexander's Grecian Kingdom would be divided four ways among his generals. The Seleucids would partially gain control of the Middle East region, and eventually one of these descendants would commit the Abomination of Desolation in the Temple of Jerusalem. This happened when Antiochus Epiphanes invaded Israel in 167 BC and defiled the Temple (Daniel 8:9-12). He, however, became a prototype of the final False Prophet of history! What he did was repeated in AD 70, and finally will be repeated at the end of history as we know it. We have been warned! It is this Beast, the forgotten Beast, that will ruthlessly apply the "will" of the Antichrist to the world, and he will seek more than anything to destroy Israel and thereby vanquish her God! Islam is obsessed with destroying the Jews and Israel, because until this happens it cannot claim religious supremacy or that it is the custodian of a better revelation. The God of Israel is standing in her

way! It was because of this obsession that Islamic leaders forged a working alliance with Hitler during the Second World War. Their "interests" coincided, even though their values differed. Israel has no enemy like that of Islam, and it is Islam that calls itself the religion of the prophet. Islam's present-day rise and alliance with the liberal far left of Europe is a strange but foreboding development that we would do well to take note of. Moreover, as we have previously noted, the Islamic block in the UN is seeking to pass a binding resolution that will make it a crime to criticize Islam in any way!

THE SPIRIT OF ANTICHRIST

The spirit of antichrist is a pervasive demonic influence that applies the false ideas of the Antichrist and False Prophet to the world. Also, it is a demonic "forerunner" that subverts the exclusive saving message of Jesus, thereby seeking to bring all peoples into subjection to Satan (John 2:22; 2 John 7; 2 Thessalonians 2:7-9). This "spirit" is already in the world! In recent years, its influence has grown in an accelerated fashion and can be seen by the following examples:

- The politically correct culture that is sweeping the

world today. Christians are being dismissed from their jobs for wearing crosses as pendants because, apparently, this is deeply offensive to Muslims and other peoples of faith.

- The economic chaos of our world. This is mainly manmade and will be manipulated by the "spirit of antichrist" to enslave the world.

- Acts of religious extremism, as we have recently witnessed in Norway, will be used as an excuse to limit religious freedom, redefine religious practice, and introduce a new multi-faith religious system or code that will have to be embraced and subscribed to by all peoples.

I firmly believe that another major conflict, possibly in the Middle East, will capitulate the world toward global government, a new world economic order, and the rise of super leaders. A euphoric world will celebrate peace and agree that the age of democracy is now over. A two-headed beast, looking like a lamb and a messiah, will assume control of the world and rule it by decree and supernatural signs (Revelation 13:13; 2 Thessalonians 2:9). The false prophet, or "forgotten beast," will introduce a reign of terror against the Church of the living God and eventually against

the nation of Israel, and yet "he shall come to his end, and no one will help him" (Daniel 11:45).

CHAPTER THIRTEEN
BABYLON

Rejoice over her, O heaven, and you holy apostles and prophets, for God has avenged you on her!

Revelation 18:20

The final great "sign player" on the end-time field of play is Babylon. The Book of Revelation dedicates two whole chapters, 18 and 19, to the subject, thereby giving us an idea of the importance that it should hold for us. Our understanding of the term goes back to the Book of Genesis where, in chapter 11, we find humankind uniting and pooling its resources to build a tower that in its mind is testimony to their god-like status and to its rejection of the God of the Bible. Humankind determines its own destiny and does not need the interference of God in this matter!

It can reach the heavens, achieve anything it desires, and therefore it will remove the shackles of belief in God from its agenda. Sadly, this is all deception of the worst kind, and it is ultimately fickle and sourced out of gross spiritual blindness. Thus humankind's ingenuity knows no boundaries but will unleash great wickedness and evil on the world. Rebellion against God has changed the human heart from light to darkness, and thus it employs its ingenuity in the pursuit of evil. John's Gospel puts it this way:

> *And this is the condemnation, that light has come into the world, and men loved darkness rather than light, because their deeds were evil.*
>
> John 3:19

GLOBALIZATION

The story of Babylon is really that of humankind's determination to bring about a one-world financial system and government. Globalization is therefore not a new phenomenon but an ancient one, and it is still inherently wicked! God well knew its dangers:

> *And the LORD said, "Indeed the people are one and*

they all have one language, and this is what they begin to do; now nothing that they purpose to do will be withheld from them. Come let Us go down and there confuse their language, that they may not understand one another's speech."

Genesis 11:6-7

A world in rebellion against God should not be allowed to unite, but this is the strategy of the devil! Globalization is a pathway to what I call brilliant evil. The tower of Babel was indeed a marvel, just as the ill-fated Titanic was. In fact, the construction of this ship was heralded as a new age for mankind, but God also looked down from heaven and "toppled it," just as he had done some four thousand years before Christ! Since the fall of Babylon, the powers of darkness have clawed their way back to a new Babylon. It's being built right before our eyes. So Babylon stands for many things, all of them wicked, and the God of Heaven is against it. He brought confusion to those who embarked upon its road. They spoke many tongues, divided, and went their way, but the devil never stopped planning and plotting. He wants globalization at all costs so that by it, and through it, he can unleash a tidal wave of evil against the human race. Indeed the very word Babylon represents ev-

erything that opposes God; therefore, the great Empire of Babylon is pictured in the Bible as the great enemy of the people of God.

In Daniel's time it was regional—east of Israel—but now it has grown to become a world system. It spread through Rome, called Babylon in the New Testament (1 Peter 5:13), and eventually became a worldwide entity just before Jesus' second coming. This is the picture painted for us in Revelation 17 and 18. These chapters warn us about all of this, and we should take note.

MYSTICAL BABYLON

Revelation 17 introduces us to the mystical side of Babylon. It is a false religious system, grounded in the occult, that seeks to deceive the world. It even infiltrates the Church and induces it to murder true followers of Jesus (2 Corinthians 11:12-15). John is shocked because he realizes that what he is seeing is so-called Christians killing true Christians in the name of Jesus! He thus sees a giant apostate Church appearing on the stage of history that is "drunk with the blood of the martyrs" (Revelation 17:6). Rightly is it named "the great harlot" (Revelation 17:1). This "harlot woman" is in league with a global agenda and thus forms

an alliance with the coming "Beast" or Antichrist. She is adorned with purple, gold, and scarlet and enjoys worldly prestige but is, in fact, a fornicating harlot in God's eyes. She will deny that Jesus is the only way of salvation and will ride with the Beast into war against the people of God. God describes her thus:

> MYSTERY, BABYLON THE GREAT, THE MOTHER OF HARLOTS AND OF THE ABOMINATIONS OF THE EARTH.
>
> Revelation 17:5

We would do well to take note because I believe that this harlot church is very much alive today. Great church movements that once preached a true Gospel have abandoned this message in favor of a politically correct one that validates other religious systems. This "fornicating gospel" has infiltrated all historical church traditions, even those that came out of the Reformation. The Word of God is being attacked, its veracity is being questioned and those who stand up for the truth are vilified as bigots. Some evangelical churches of great fame are uniting with Muslims, holding meetings together, declaring that both groups serve the same god and are even giving themselves a new name;

Chrislam! The world will applaud this, and a one-world government led by a charismatic and very able individual will fully endorse it and actually use it to gain control of the masses. Mystical Babylon will impact the whole earth! John writes, "Then he said to me, 'The waters which you saw, where the Harlot sits, are peoples, multitudes, nations and tongues'" (Revelation 17:15).

Note that Babylon always brings "tongues" together! Indeed, the only way in which "tongues can be brought together," free from evil, is when men and women are saved by the spilt blood of Jesus and filled with the Spirit! On the Day of Pentecost, the Spirit of God fell upon the waiting disciples in the Upper Room, and they spoke in the many tongues of men. Those who heard were amazed and could not understand how this could be.

> *And when this sound occurred, the multitude came together and were confused, because everyone heard them speak in his own language. Then they were all amazed and marveled, saying to one another, "Look, are not all these who speak Galileans? And how is it that we hear, each in our own language in which we were born."*
>
> Acts 2:6-8

The message is clear: without God our tongues are a

source of great evil, and they can only be tamed by the Holy Spirit. James knew this well and wrote, "even so the tongue is a little member and boasts of great things. See how great a forest a little fire kindles! And the tongue is a fire . . . set on fire by hell!" (James 3:5-6). The tongues of men, not restrained by God Himself, will bring the "fire" of Babylon to the world!

Once the "harlot church," like a useful idiot, has served the purposes of the Beast, he will destroy it and set up his global religious system that will be linked to the global financial system (Revelation 17:16). The trap will be complete, Babylon will have emerged again, and all tongues will in glorious unity, just as the Germans worshipped Hitler, worship the Beast (Revelation 13:11, 15-17).

THE TRIUMPH OF JESUS

Mystical Babylon is growing around us with every passing day. More and more, Jesus is being driven from the main street of life, and people everywhere are being seduced by Babylon's false religious ideas. From New Age theories to the United Nation's World Parliament of Religions, we see this spirit infiltrating the world. The awful wars spawned by religious systems, including deluded Christian

ones, have all helped endorse the call for a new and only global religious system. This false global system will be in place when Jesus comes again; it awaits us. He will defeat it when He comes, and our chapter puts it this way:

> *These will make war with the Lamb and the Lamb will overcome them, for He is Lord of Lords and King of Kings; and those who are with Him are called, chosen and faithful.*
>
> Revelation 17:14

The question is, "Are you with Him?" Those who are called and chosen will share in His triumph. Scripture exhorts us to make sure of our election and calling (2 Peter 1:10). This means putting Jesus first in everything and avoiding the pitfalls of "Mystical Babylon."

COMMERCIAL BABYLON

Chapter 18 introduces us to Commercial Babylon. Babylon, as we have seen, is more than a false religious system. It is indeed a religious/political/commercial system that by the end of time enslaves the world, but it has always been here enticing the people of God to serve "things" more than they serve God. The Bible calls this loving the world

(1 John 2:15-17). God hates this, as it really has nothing to do with what you do but rather with a malady of the heart. Scripture refers to this malady as "the lust of the flesh, the lust of the eyes and the boastful pride of life" (1 John2:16). Or as the adage goes, worldliness is the desire for "girls, gold, and glory!" That is, worldliness is loving something more than you love Jesus. It could also be a pursuit that is quite legitimate, but in your—or my—case, evil, because it gains more of our time, energy, and resources than Jesus does! So a worldly person could be a faithful church attendee, who dresses neatly, pays tithes and even serves where possible but actually loves his or her career more than Jesus! God really opposes those who give way to this problem. In this regard, James writes:

> *Adulterers and adulteresses! Do you not know that friendship with the world is enmity with God? Whoever therefore wants to be a friend of the world makes himself an enemy of God.*
>
> James 4:4

Babylon is subtle and clever, as it deceives and undermines the faith of some by endeavors that are not inherently wicked. Of course it involves everything that is evil and

wrong, but it lays a snare for the people of God, and before they know it they love golf, their careers, hobbies, and family more than they love Jesus. The only remedy is, "Come out of her, my people, lest you share in her sins, and lest you receive of her plagues" (Revelation 18:4).

FOOD FOR THOUGHT

Revelation 18 introduces us to a long list of commercial endeavors (verses 9-20). It is quite remarkable, because this list includes the "souls of men" (verse 13). If we allow Babylon to attract us, we will sell our souls just as we trade bronze, iron, marble, precious stones, wood, wine, fine linen, gold, silver, and many other things. This is not a game; many have sold their very souls for these things and thereby gone to eternal destruction. Babylon is constantly knocking at your door, and you will have to ward it off repeatedly. Jesus knew this and said, "For what profit is it to a man if he gains the whole world, and loses his own soul? What will a man give in exchange for his soul?" (Matthew 16:26). Truly these are two very good questions that constitute much food for thought.

The Apostle Paul reflected on these things in his second epistle to the believers at Corinth. The church had

been riddled with carnal behavior; some of it of the worst kind. The real problem was that many in the church had a "heart problem." They had allowed other interests and things to supplant their love for Christ. As Paul closes his letter he urges them to examine their hearts so as to determine whether they really are saved! This is indeed a good thing to do and we should think about this as well. Following Jesus is more than just taking out "fire insurance." It's about loving God with all our hearts, minds, souls and strength (Mark 12:29-30). So, let's read Paul's words again and use them as food for thought:

> *Examine yourselves as to whether you are in the faith. Test yourselves. Do you not know yourselves, that Jesus Christ is in you?—unless indeed you are disqualified.*
>
> 2 Corinthians 13:5

CHAPTER FOURTEEN

SPECIAL DEVOTION

Called and Chosen

MATTHEW 13:47-52

Jesus told a remarkable parable that, if we stop to think about it, would "sharpen" our spiritual lives. It is the parable of the dragnet. Matthew 13 is that great chapter of his Gospel wherein he records the various parables of the Kingdom of God. A parable is a story or illustration that is designed to highlight one simple truth about the Kingdom of God. Jesus frequently used the parabolic method in His preaching because it made people think, and only those who thought through the story carefully would get its message. In other words, it was designed to "catch" the spiritually hungry. The twelve Disciples often thought through the parable and even asked Jesus for clarity

(Mark 4:10-13). Those who had no such desire would give up, turn away and follow Him no more. Jesus was not really interested in great numbers. He was "fishing" for the elect—that is, those who were called and would become chosen. A parable attracted "the called," and their final response would determine whether they were chosen (Matthew 20:16). Jesus told Paul to preach without fear in Corinth, as He had many thirsty people in that city and wanted them, through preaching, to be called (Acts 18:9-10).

All this is very interesting and challenging, and it teaches us several things:

1 **We should be spiritually hungry all the time.** We all know what it feels like to be thirsty. The thirst overtakes all your desires and thinking, and it will not be satisfied until it has been quenched. We are to have a perpetual spiritual thirst. In fact, when we have it, it introduces us to the wonderful, mysterious, and satisfying truths of the Kingdom of God. If we do not "protect our thirst" and thus ensure that it is sustained, even what we have, in terms of understanding the wonders of the Kingdom of God, will be taken from us! Jesus put it this way: "For whoever

has, to him more will be given, and he will have abundance; but whoever does not have, even what he has will be taken away from him" (Matthew 13:12).

This is quite terrifying, because it teaches us that if we are not going forward in our spiritual growth, we will be going backward with heavenly help! The question is, do we thirst for the things of God? Or better still, do we want an abundance of heavenly revelation? The answer should be yes. Jesus Himself taught that a meaningful and powerful relationship with the Holy Spirit is conditional upon our being thirsty (John 7:37-39).

2 **We should be called and chosen.** The parable of the dragnet sees people as fish caught in a net and then drawn to the shore. They are all called and are in one huge bundle, but eventually they are sorted out and only a few become chosen. If we are not careful to protect our thirst for spiritual things, our spiritual lives will decay and corrode, even though they started out with such promise. Paul writes that trusted followers of Jesus, and even preachers, eventually made "shipwrecks" of their lives (1 Timothy 1:19). This imagery is shocking, as

it conjures up the picture of a once-beautiful sailing ship being smashed to pieces on the rocks near the shoreline. This is no game or hypothetical theory—many who once rejoiced in the house of God have gone this way. They were called but were not in the end chosen, all because they lost their thirst!

3 **We should live in the expectation of Jesus' Second Coming.** The consummation of the age, which is brought about by the second coming of Jesus, will witness the great separation of the people of God. The called and chosen look alike to us, but not to God! There will be some great surprises as we witness those whom we deemed to be chosen designated "the wicked" and cast into the furnace of hell! As Jesus comes forth from Heaven in great glory and power, His angels will go out to the four corners of the Earth, gathering His chosen from the "same playing field" as the wicked. They will rise to meet Him in the air but the "look-alike" called will be left. Their destiny is awful, to say the least, but they have only themselves to blame. They were called and invited to become the chosen; they heard the call and came but then lost their thirst and turned

away, relying on decent living, churchgoing, and the right language to guarantee their eternal destiny. It will not work! Jesus asked His Disciples, "Have you understood all these things?" (Matthew 13:51). This is the question He puts to us today. I wonder how we are answering it.

4 **We should store in the safe spiritual locker of our hearts the treasures of the Kingdom of God.** God gives us revelation to impart. As we thirst and receive, we do not forget, and as time goes by, we will bring "out of his treasure things new and old" (Matthew 13:52). Note that things new come before things old, implying a constant reception of new truth and revelation. In other words, the wise disciple of the Kingdom of God imparts life to others and, depending on where his target audience is spiritually, he shares with them the treasures of Heaven that he has received. Blessed is this disciple, and, more important still, he is wise. How wise are we?

The parables of the Kingdom of Heaven are incredible, and we are to think carefully about them. God speaks in parables all the time (Psalm 79:2) and thereby He invites us

to share in fellowship with Him. The truth is, God wants a family in every sense of the word, and this family must share His life, values, and purpose. There can be no substitute for a family relationship with Him. He is not interested in religion or ritual but in our hearts, and these He wants to captivate fully.

CHAPTER FIFTEEN

GENERAL DESCRIPTIONS

Great and marvelous are Your works, Lord God Almighty! Just and true are Your ways, O King of the saints! Who shall not fear You, O Lord and glorify Your name? For all nations shall come and worship before You, for Your judgments have been manifested.

Revelation 15:3-4

Chapters 14 and 15 of the Book of Revelation are general descriptions of the end-time events. That is, they give greater insight into the information that has been given, especially in respect to the great sign chapters of the book. In a way, they fill in the gaps and help us to understand more fully the issues at hand.

Of major importance is the assertion of the sovereignty of God and the certain triumph of Jesus over all that is wicked and evil in these chapters. The reader must know and understand all the important characters and issues that will unfold on Earth as we approach the second coming of Jesus without getting sidetracked and taking his or her spiritual gaze off Jesus. He is working His purpose in the Earth, and we must continue to glorify Him. In short, the detail is important, otherwise the Holy Spirit would not have given it, but we must not get "bogged down" in it. God is, and will remain, in control of His world!

THE SPIRITUAL VIRGINS

Chapter 14 opens with a scene that depicts the 144,000 saints standing before the throne of God; they are swept up in praise to God, praise so great that it sounds like mighty thunder! These, we are told, have been "redeemed from the earth" (verse 3). They enjoy a unique relationship with Christ in heaven and therefore are always at His side (verse 4). Many believe that these are Jewish believers because of the information given in chapter 7. This is true, but not exclusively, as the number 144,000 is in fact the number of government, or fullness, in the Bible. So in

its pages we read of twelve tribes of Israel, twelve Apostles, twelve baskets full of "leftovers," twelve gates to the heavenly city, twenty-four heavenly elders at the throne of God, and multiples of twelve relating to the redeemed of God (144,000). In other words the term signifies abundance and fullness and, as it relates to the redeemed, it refers to God's perfect rule over millions of people, from all the earth, who have been redeemed by the blood of the Lamb. Our faith is essentially Jewish in root and character (Romans 11:17), and as Gentiles, we have been grafted into spiritual Israel. As Paul put it in Galatians 6:16, we are the "Israel of God," though redeemed from every tribe and tongue on the face of the Earth. If we keep ourselves pure and holy for Jesus, we shall be His bride and we will be presented to Him as spiritual virgins (Revelation 14:4). Paul echoes this thought when he writes that Jesus will present to Himself the Church "without spot or wrinkle or any such thing" (Ephesians 5:27). This is the calling and promise that is set before us!

THE DANGERS OF THE BEAST

Chapter 14 also contains a threefold angelic proclamation that asserts the sovereign creative power of God, His

judgments over the Earth, and His warnings to the Church not to embrace the intimidation and wickedness of the Beast government, as those who do will share the same destiny as this wicked entity. The late nineteenth century and the twentieth century witnessed the emergence of three systems of belief that have attacked the existence of God and thereby advanced the influence of the spirit of antichrist greatly in the world. I am referring to Darwinism, Communism, and Secularism. These three "isms" have infiltrated the minds of people everywhere—especially young people—in different ways and modes, but the effect has been the same: the removal of God from our world. The schools in the West have been greatly affected by these ills, and thus evolution has become the only acceptable theory of creation, prayer and Bible reading have been banned, and man is presented as the center of all things and the determiner of his own destiny. Those who believe otherwise are branded as fundamentalists, and people who claim to know God and speak to Him are laughed at and considered delusional. This chapter gives a warning to the Church and the world! Concerning creation, it states:

Fear God and give glory to Him, for the hour of His judgment has come; and worship Him who made

heaven and earth, the sea and springs of water.

Revelation 14:7

Concerning the antichrist Beast political system it warns:

If anyone worships the beast and his image, and receives his mark on his forehead or on his hand, he himself shall also drink of the wine of the wrath of God, which is poured out full strength into the cup of His indignation. He shall be tormented with fire and brimstone in the presence of the holy angels and in the presence of the Lamb.

Revelation 14:9-10

And, concerning the secular world, which damns people's souls by all that gratifies the lusts of men:

Babylon is fallen, is fallen, that great city, because she has made all nations drink of the wine of the wrath of her fornication."

Revelation 14:8

The only hope for our dying world is the Gospel of Jesus. Every nation, tribe, and tongue needs it, and behind

its proclamation on Earth are great Angels who watch over its message and reach (verse 6). Those who embrace it will find themselves in conflict with a world system that opposes everything they stand for. But to be judged, this system must be revealed for what it is. The enemies of God will come out into the open, to "Jesus' footstool," and He will not come again until this happens. However, this will mean great trials for the people of God; they will have to patiently endure, knowing all the while that the day of their eternal and blessed deliverance is coming. So John hears a proclamation that states:

> *Here is the patience of the saints; here are those who keep the commandments of God and the faith of Jesus. Then I heard a voice from heaven saying to me, "Write: 'Blessed are the dead who die in the Lord from now on.'"*
>
> *"Yes," says the Spirit, "that they may rest from their labors, and their works follow them."*
>
> Revelation 14:12-13

THE DAY OF THE LORD

The remaining part of the chapter focuses our attention on the Day of the Lord. Two things happen on that awesome Day, as we have already noted: Jesus descends from Heaven with His mighty angels, in flaming fire (2 Thessalonians 1:6-8), and His church is "reaped" from across the world (Revelation 14:14-16). It is changed in a twinkling of an eye (1 Corinthians 15:52) and, by supernatural power, rises to meet the Son of Man as He comes (1 Thessalonians 4:13-17). What a wonderful day this will be, and to endure until its coming will be worth it all, because our "light affliction" is storing up for us an "eternal weight of glory" (2 Corinthians 4:17).

The ungodly will have nowhere to hide or to run. They will call out to the mountains to fall on them as they witness the approaching war horse of the Son of God (Revelation 6:15-17). Having rejected the grace of God, in the Gospel of Jesus, they will have no hope and no help. Like ripened grapes, they will fall under the wrath of God, His mighty wine-press, in their millions and go to hell (Revelation 14:17-20)! Their blood will run like rivers, and their ungodly pursuits will be remembered no more. Jude also saw this Day and wrote:

Now Enoch, the seventh from Adam, prophesied about these men also, saying, "Behold, the Lord comes with ten thousand of His saints, to execute judgment on all, to convict all who are ungodly among them of all their ungodly deeds which they have committed in an ungodly way, and of all the harsh things which ungodly sinners have spoken against Him."

Jude 1:14-15

THE SONG OF THE OVERCOMERS

As the judgments of God continue to strike an unrepentant world, the believers who have endured the wrath of Antichrist and his demonic system are seen finally in heaven (Revelation 15:1-2). Their reward is great, for they have stood fast and have not denied the faith. They are appropriately honored, and as they gather before the throne of God, they sing the "Song of Moses" (verses 3-4). This is once again the principle of remez. That is, it is a reference to Deuteronomy 32, where we find the full account of the song. We must ask the question, "Why is it so important?" The answer is because it gives a detailed outline of all of redemption history, from the very beginning to the very end! Moses, like Abraham, understood the full redemptive

initiative, including everything to do with Jesus' first coming, atonement, and second coming. Jesus Himself acknowledged this (see John 5:45-47)! Thus chapter 32 of Deuteronomy can be divided up as follows:

- A eulogy to the greatness of God and His just ways; verses 1-4.
- A recognition of the sin and weakness of His people Israel; verses 5-6.
- A call to remember His choice and calling over Israel, His inheritance; verses 7-9.
- A reminder of God's care for Israel in the desert after He called them out of Egypt; verses 10-12.
- A description of the blessings of the Promised Land; verses 11-14.
- A chronicle of Israel's rebellion against God; verses 15-18.
- A description of Israel's blindness; verses 19-20
- A divine decision to provoke Israel to jealousy by God's reaching out to the Gentiles; verses 21-22.

- A commitment to send Israel into exile as an instrument of divine correction; verses 23-33.
- A promise of restoration through correction; verses 34-42.
- A day of salvation for Israel that will be rejoiced in by the saved Gentile peoples; verse 43.

It is therefore clear that way back in the five books of Moses we have outlined for us the eternal purpose of God as it unfolds on the Earth. This is the plan and the only plan that God ever had, and He gave it to us more than three thousand years ago. As we approach the end of the age, with all its struggles and trials, we can be sure of this one thing: at the end we will all sing the "Song of Moses" before the throne of God and marvel at God's just ways and sovereignty over the Earth! The Beast and all his dark hordes really accomplish Jesus' purpose as they unleash their blind hatred of all things good on the earth. No wonder the redeemed of Israel and the nations will sing:

> *Great and marvelous are Your works, Lord God Almighty! Just and true are Your ways, O King of the saints! Who shall not fear You, O Lord, and glorify your name? For you alone are holy. For all nations shall come*

and worship before You, for Your judgments have been manifested.

Revelation 15:3-4

It is to be noted that the positive emphasis that the Book of Revelation places on the saints who endure and triumph over the Beast constitutes serious food for thought. Throughout the Book, the "tribulation saints" are eulogized and praised by the God of heaven. But more than this, they are rewarded with a special place in relationship to Jesus throughout eternity (Revelation 7:9-17; 15:2). Oddly, pre-tribulation rapture proponents would have us believe that these saints are not part of the church, and indeed, in many cases, were backslidden believers who didn't make "the cut" at the rapture before the Great Tribulation. I think not!

CHAPTER SIXTEEN

THE REVELATION OF JESUS CHRIST

Now I saw heaven opened, and behold, a white horse. And He who sat on him was called Faithful and True, and in righteousness He judges and makes war.

Revelation 19:11

We have now come to the great climax of the book: the Revelation of Jesus! Babylon has fallen, the wickedness of the world has come out into the open, the rebellion of humankind against God has been laid bare, and the works of the Devil have been exposed (Revelation 19:1-6). There is no place to hide; the stage is now fully set and all the players have assumed their places. The Day of the Lord has arrived! The despised followers of Jesus, of

all ages, are resurrected, and before them is a day of great rejoicing as they get ready to celebrate the marriage supper of the Lamb! As the luminaries change, the resurrected believers are supernaturally lifted into the heavens to meet Jesus as He descends on a great white horse of war. Still reverberating in the ears of the saints is the great shout and trumpet blast of the archangel, and dazzling in great splendor before them is the specter of Jesus, who they are now seeing visibly for the first time (2 Thessalonians 1:7-10). What a Day this will be!

The chapter has three sections: The Marriage Supper of the Lamb and the Judgment of Believers, The Revelation of Jesus, and The End of the Beast.

THE MARRIAGE SUPPER OF THE LAMB AND THE JUDGMENT OF BELIEVERS

The passage opens with a shout of triumph as the Bride of Christ prepares for the second coming of Jesus. Hers is an exclamation of expectation as she will now be scrutinized or judged, rewarded, and presented to her Groom. He will make her His own, and with her, reign over the earth (Revelation 5:10)! Her bridal gown is not a robe of righteousness but a robe of reward. It is symbolic of her

"righteous acts" (Revelation 19:8). For all eternity, it will be a testament to the believer's love and dedication to Jesus while he or she was on earth. The whole scene is one of excitement, victory, worship, and heavenly joy. Those in heaven and at the throne of God are filled with wonder as they hear a voice exclaim, "Praise our God, all you His servants and those who fear Him, both small and great" (Revelation 19:5).

The Judgment of Believers and the Marriage Supper of the Lamb takes place on earth in Jerusalem. Because of the cataclysmic upheavals of the Day of the Lord, Jerusalem, after a great earthquake, will be elevated and restored to incredible beauty. Isaiah, the great Hebrew Prophet, writes, "Now it shall come to pass in the latter days that the mountain of the LORD's house shall be established on the top of the mountains, and shall be exalted above the hills; and all nations shall flow to it" (Isaiah 2:2). In addition Zechariah, the restoration Prophet, writes of the Day of the Lord and Jesus' second coming, seeing the same elevation of Jerusalem but with this addition: she will be a sea port (Zechariah 14:3-10)! Moreover, Haggai, another restoration Prophet, writes of the beauty of Jerusalem by calling it the "Desire of All Nations" (Haggai 2:7).

Isaiah has a remarkable prophetic view of things; he

sees the very end of the age when death is swallowed up in victory and thus banished from the redeemed human experience, and when the Lord God of Heaven, Jesus, the Son of the living God, gathers His bride on the elevated hills of Jerusalem for a great banquet: the Marriage Supper of the Lamb!

> *And in this mountain the LORD of hosts will make for all people a feast of choice pieces, a feast of wines on the lees, of fat things full of marrow, of well-refined wines on the lees. And He will destroy on this mountain the surface of the covering cast over all people, and the veil that is spread over all nations. He will swallow up death forever, And the Lord God will wipe away tears from all faces; the rebuke of His people He will take away from all the earth; for the LORD has spoken.*
>
> Isaiah 25:6-8

We all have a remarkable destiny, and it will unfold with Jesus in Jerusalem! Not only will we feast with Him at the great Marriage Supper of the Lamb, but we will rule and reign with Him over the nations (Revelation 19:15; 2:25-27). This first part of Revelation 19 concludes with an assertion of Jesus' divinity. We are to worship Him and not created beings of any type (verse 10).

THE REVELATION OF JESUS

No words can really describe the glory and magnificence of this passage. Heaven is "opened"; the visible and invisible worlds merge, as Jesus descends on a white horse of war with thousands upon thousands of angels accompanying Him. Like vast clouds, His elect, from the four corners of the Earth, are caught up to meet and greet Him as He comes in triumph! The scene is breathtaking. When Jesus first called His disciples, He told them about this day—while they marveled at His supernatural wisdom and knowledge, He affirmed that they were destined to see heaven opened one day with angels ascending and descending upon the Son of Man (John 1:50-51). That "day" is fast approaching! Here, however, in Revelation 19, the picture is one of blessedness if redeemed, and therefore one of His children. But if not, it is a terrifying one as it is all about war, wrath, and overwhelming flames of fire. Much of what John sees here is exactly how he saw Jesus in Chapter 1. The spiritual presentation of Jesus to His Church is now the physical presentation of Jesus to a godless world! Jesus comes forth out of heaven to make war and John describes Him thus:

> *His eyes were like a flame of fire, and on His head were many crowns. He had a name written that no one knew except Himself. He was clothed with a robe dipped in blood, and His name is called The Word of God. And the armies in heaven, clothed in fine linen, white and clean, followed Him on white horses. Now out of His mouth goes a sharp sword, that with it He should strike the nations...*
>
> Revelation 19:12-15

Most important of all is the fact that He is coming to assume His rightful place in Israel and the world. He is the "KING OF KINGS AND LORD OF LORDS." A world that has routinely rejected Him is now about to be judged as He "treads the winepress of the fierceness and wrath of Almighty God." The promise that God gave in Psalm 2 that He would install His king on Mount Zion is fulfilled, and the nations are without excuse. They have rejected the love of God and now bear the consequences. The grace of God has ended, the "door of the ark" has been closed, and there is nowhere to run and hide!

THE END OF THE BEAST

A primary focus of Jesus' return to Earth is the capture of the Beast and the False Prophet. These two evil beings are apprehended and thrown alive into the lake of fire that burns eternally (Revelation 19:19-21). Once again, it is to be noted that time and time again in this amazing book our attention is drawn to the rise, power, evil, and awful end of the Beast! Chapter after chapter warns us of his arrival and demonic activities. This is not for nothing. How sad it is that so many in the modern-day church have been seduced into believing that they will never be around to witness the rise of Antichrist, even though Scripture affirms that his rise will require courage and patience from the saints (Revelation 13:10; 14:12). This seduction has weakened the Church and left it unprepared! When he comes, many will fall away, being quite unable to face up to his tyranny. Jesus Himself warned in His Olivet Discourse that, because of the "pressure" in the end time, "the love of many would grow cold" (Matthew 24:12). He relates this directly to the rise of false Christs and false prophets. I am constantly reminded of the words of Paul, recorded in 2 Thessalonians 2:5, where, after warning them about the arrival of Antichrist, he states that when he was with them on a previous

occasion, "I told you these things." John the Apostle does the same thing in his first epistle when he writes, "Little children, it is the last hour; and as you have heard that the Antichrist is coming, even now many antichrists have come, by which we know that it is the last hour" (2:18). Having said this, he then goes on to state that they will discern him and thus be forewarned, because they "have an anointing from the Holy One, and you know all things" (2:20). Why would he bother if he knew that they were to be whisked away to safety before the reign of the Beast?

Likewise, the Book of Revelation is warning us, and the Holy Spirit wants us to know, that while the reign of the Beast will be terrible, if we hold true, One far greater in power and splendor is coming who will defeat the Beast and establish righteousness in the earth and reign with us over it! He is THE KING OF KINGS AND LORD OF LORDS.

CHAPTER SEVENTEEN

SPECIAL DEVOTION

Times and Seasons

But concerning the times and the seasons, brethren, you have no need that I should write to you. For you yourselves know perfectly that the day of the Lord so comes as a thief in the night. . . . But you, brethren, are not in darkness, so that this Day should overtake you as a thief.

1 Thessalonians 5:1-2, 4

JESUS' WORDS

It is clear from Jesus' words that no man knows the day of His return (Mark 13:32). However, the "season of His return" is discerned by His Church. This is the clear intention of Jesus' Olivet Discourse, and it is worthy to note that Jesus is definitely

not coming "as a thief" for His Church but for the world. Paul underlines this in 1 Thessalonians. It is not good enough to say, "Get ready no matter what." If this were true, then why would the Spirit of God go to the trouble of giving us so much detail about the end time in His inspired Word? I for one am quite tired of people laughing about the Book of Revelation and passing it off with a statement that discounts it and gives the impression that it can all be forgotten and neglected. This, in my opinion, grieves the Holy Spirit and says more about our ignorance of God's Word than anything else! Quite frankly, then, to disregard these vast passages of the Bible is arrogant, irreverent, and displeasing to God. We must be prepared, as this will help us settle life and death issues when they arise. The whole purpose of the Book of Revelation is to prepare the Church for what is coming. If you don't know the nature of your enemy, how will you be able to resist Him? Being "ready" without appropriate preparation will leave you in the dark, unable to defend yourself.

DANIEL'S WORDS

Daniel 9 introduces us to the concept of what theologians call "Daniel's Seventieth Week" (Daniel 9:24-27).

Daniel is told that seventy weeks are set aside by which God will restore Jerusalem, bring in the Messiah of Israel, and bring a conclusion to His redemptive purpose on the earth. These are weeks of years—that is, 490 years, from the decree to rebuild Jerusalem, would pass until the redemptive plan of God would be fully accomplished. After sixty-nine weeks (seven weeks and sixty-two weeks), or 483 years, the Messiah would come and die. Jesus actually came and died exactly 483 years after a decree went forth from Artexerses the Second in 445 BC, giving instruction to rebuild Jerusalem and its temple. The Jewish people thus knew the exact date of their Messiah's coming. This is amazing! Their rejection of Jesus' Messianic credentials did two things:

1 It brought Gentiles into the spiritual house of Israel (Ephesians 3:3-7; Romans 11:17-24).

2 It delayed the fulfillment of the final seven years, Daniel's Seventieth Week, of redemptive history.

Much of Daniel's writings have to do with this final seven years (week) of human history as we know it. The

same is true of the Book of Revelation. Both books refer to this period as "a time and times and half a time," as "1260 days," or as "forty-two months." Naturally two of these periods equal seven years (Daniel 7:25; Revelation 13:5; 11:3). It also appears from both books that this final period of seven years begins after the restoration of the Jewish people to the land of Israel and the signing of a peace agreement that finally settles the so-called Middle East conflict (Daniel 9:27). The Beast rises to power by achieving what many leaders, scholars, presidents, and politicians could not do. He brings the Arab/Israeli conflict to an end and does so by guaranteeing Israel's existence and sovereign boundaries. He will be greeted with global jubilation, and even Israel will herald him a leader of leaders! It is this same individual that after 1260 days sets up the "Abomination of Desolation" in the Temple and who will finally be overcome and destroyed by Jesus at His second coming (Daniel 11:31; 2 Thessalonians 2:3-8).

Daniel further helps us to pinpoint this period in history by stating that these great end-time events will take place at a time when "many shall run to and fro, and knowledge shall increase" (Daniel 12:4). It is incredible to think that just over a hundred years ago, humankind was still using horse-drawn carriages as its primary means of

transport. Today we travel into outer space, have orbiting space stations above us, and step into jet planes that transport us across the world in less than a day while we watch movies, enjoy delicious meals, and buy discounted gifts for our friends and family. Herein is the collision of knowledge with amazing machines of travel. Talk about "those wonderful men in their flying machines." The end-time has arrived! Be prepared and spiritually brace yourself for what is coming; the rise of the Beast. According to John, he will "make war with the saints . . . and overcome them" (Revelation 13:7).

PAUL'S WORDS

While Paul has much to say about the "times and seasons," he gives one singular warning in the second chapter of 2 Thessalonians that Jesus is not coming back for His Church until two final signs appear in the world. The two signs are a great falling away from the Church of the living God and the arrival of the Beast, or, as he puts it, "the son of perdition" (2 Thessalonians 2:1-3). It is my belief that the overwhelming pressure and struggles of the days just ahead of us will cause many Christians to turn away and leave the faith. This is exactly what happened in the great

persecutions against the Church in the first 250 years of its fledgling history. Many Christians faced with the hostility of Rome gave up, denied their faith, and fell away. Why would it be different now? Also, when the Beast steps onto the stage of world history, the real "hour of testing" will have arrived, and with it the consummation of the age. Jesus promised never to leave His people through it all (Matthew 28:20).

In closing this devotional, it is worth noting that Jesus warned that the coming events will be so threatening to the very existence of the human race that His Father would have to shorten the days (Mark 13:20). This is an added reason to appreciate that no one will know the day of Jesus' return. However, we do know the season, and it's time to be prepared and, as Jesus put it, watch!

CHAPTER EIGHTEEN

DAYS OF RESURRECTION, BLESSING, AND JUDGMENT

Blessed and holy is he who has part in the first resurrection. Over such the second death has no power, but they shall be priests of God and Christ, and shall reign with Him a thousand years.

Revelation 20:6

When Jesus returns to Earth, He will set up a remarkable kingdom that at the outset will be free of all demonic influence. The Devil will be bound with his hordes of demons and cast into the bottomless pit (Revelation 20:1-3). No longer will he be free to deceive the nations. He will be bound for a thousand years. With this reality, we are introduced to the thousand-year reign

of Jesus on the Earth. Scripture, as we have seen a number of times, teaches that Jesus is destined to rule the nations "with a rod of iron" (Isaiah 11:4; Revelation 2:26-27; 12:5). Theologically, this period is also known as the Millennium or Messianic Age. It is a time that many dictators and kings have tried to establish but have miserably failed, because of their carnality and wickedness. Hitler, with his idea of setting up a Third Reich, was the most recent leader to attempt this. His failure brought with it the destruction of fifty-three million people. The true Messianic Age will be set up by Christ when the nations that have survived the Day of the Lord will be brought under Jesus' rule, and that of a resurrected Church from an elevated Jerusalem. The Book of Psalms looks forward to this day as David, some three thousand years ago, wrote of it.

> *I will declare the decree: The Lord has said to Me, "You are My Son, today I have begotten You. Ask of Me, and I will give You the nations for Your inheritance, and the ends of the earth for Your possession. You shall break them with a rod of iron; You shall dash them to pieces like a potter's vessel."*
>
> Psalm 2:7-9

THE TRUE NEW WORLD ORDER

The New World Order that Jesus will set up will be characterized by the following:

1 It will be a period of peace such as the world has never known or experienced before. Wars and conflict will be a thing of the past (Isaiah 2:1-4; 9:6).

2 It will be a time when the natural temperament of the animal kingdom will be "tamed," and therefore the most wild and dangerous of animals will no longer be aggressive. Scripture affirms that the "wolf also shall dwell with the lamb, the leopard shall lie down with the young goat, the calf and the young lion and the fatling together; and a little child will lead them" (Isaiah 11:6; 65:24-25).

3 It will be a season when all nations will rejoice in the manifest goodness and glory of God, and they will ascend annually to Jerusalem to celebrate the Feast of Tabernacles (Isaiah 11:9; Zechariah 14:16-17).

4 During this age, the natural world of fauna and flora will be transformed and become what God originally intended it to be (Romans 8:18-22). There will be spectacular natural beauty all over the earth!

5 The thousand-year reign of Jesus will forever vindicate the Church and the role that Israel has played out in history for the sake of God's plan of world redemption (Revelation 2:26-29; Ezekiel 36:1-15; Isaiah 60:12).

6 It will vindicate Jesus and set Him up as King of Kings and Lord of Lords (Revelation 11:15).

The nature of Jesus' New World Order is beautifully described in Isaiah. Here we read:

His delight is in the fear of the Lord, and He shall not judge by the sight of His eyes, nor decide by the hearing of His ears; but with righteousness He shall judge the poor, and decide with equity for the Meek of the earth; He shall strike the earth with the rod of His mouth, and with the breath of His lips He shall slay the wicked. Righteousness shall be the belt of His loins, and

faithfulness the belt of His waist.

Isaiah 11:3-5

THE TWO RESURRECTIONS OF THE DEAD

At the beginning of the Messianic Age and, as we have already seen, by the second coming of Jesus, the children of God of all ages will be resurrected, united with Christ and set apart to rule the nations with Him from an elevated Jerusalem. Scripture pronounces a blessing on all those who have a part in the first resurrection. They will live with Christ and rule and reign over the nations with Him (Revelation 20:4-6).

After the Messianic Age, the dead, both small and great, are resurrected and brought before the Great White Throne of God (Revelation 20:11-15). It is an awesome scene and it constitutes the second resurrection. They, because of their rejection of God's grace extended to them in Jesus, have no atonement for their sins, and thus they have no hope because by works they cannot gain entry to God's Kingdom (Ephesians 2:8-9). They are not blessed and even more so, because upon being judged according to their deeds, they will be justly condemned to become

part of the eternal dead! That is, they will spend eternity separated from God and in Hell. Theirs is a terrifying end that never ends and, as Scripture states, there will be much wailing and gnashing of teeth as they are cast alive, forever, into a pit of fire and brimstone! They will be clothed with bodies that will be "fire proof" and thus never be consumed by the fire and agonies to which they will be subjected. Isolated from one another and in utter darkness, they will forever lament their foolishness. Hell was never intended to house human beings, and those who go there will only have themselves to blame.

The second resurrection must and should be avoided at all costs. The only way to do this is to embrace the free offer of God's grace and love embodied in the finished work of Jesus on the cross (John 3:16). Those who do this will never perish, but those who reject the offer of God's salvation in Christ will fall eternally under the wrath of God. John wrote in his Gospel: "He who believes in the Son has everlasting life; and he who does not believe the Son shall not see life, but the wrath of God abides on him" (John 3:36).

HELL

The Bible everywhere speaks of hell, and even Jesus mentioned its reality time and time again, thus reminding us that we are all eternal beings and life does not end with physical death. In a way, it just begins because we shall cross over into an eternal state of existence. The big question is, "Where will we spend eternity, in heaven or hell?" This is a very serious question, and sadly it is not asked much today from the pulpits of our churches. One hardly even hears a message on hell today, usually because preachers do not want to upset their congregants. The neglect of the subject robs us of the whole counsel of God, removes from people a healthy fear of God, and leads many to believe that hell may not really exist at all. But it does! Here is what scripture has to say about it:

1 It is a real place (Revelation 20:13-15; Psalm 9:17; Psalm 55:15).

2 It is a place prepared uniquely for the Devil and his angels (Matthew 25:41).

3 It is a place of eternal separation from God (2 Thessalonians 1:9). This is what the Bible means by the term death.

4 It is a place that holds one captive and alive forever (Revelation 14:11).

5 It is a place where those who find themselves there will forever live under the wrath of God (Revelation 14:11). This wrath will be manifested by fire (Revelation 14:10), worms (Matthew 9:43-44; Isaiah 14:9-11), outer darkness (Matthew 8:12; 2 Peter 2:17) and demonic torment (Revelation 18:2; Revelation 9:20; Revelation 20:10).

6 It is a place to be avoided (Mark 16:16; John 3:16)!

Once again, I want to stress that, for Jesus, hell is a real place. This what He said once about it:

> *But I will show you whom you should fear: Fear Him who after He has killed has power to cast into hell; yes, I say to you fear Him!*
>
> Luke 12:5

THE FINAL DEMISE OF THE DEVIL

During the perfect, blessed reign of Jesus upon the Earth, the nations will live totally free of any demonic presence. The Bible is clear that, given the change in climate and circumstances throughout the Earth (Romans 8:18-22), people will multiply and live longer. In fact the Book of Isaiah suggests that being a hundred years old will be the usual age for a child (Isaiah 65:20)! At the end of the Messianic Age, or Millennium, the Devil will again be loosed upon the Earth to pursue once again his age-old work of deception. He will induce millions of people to rebel against God and the reign of His Son Jesus. As he did in the Garden of Eden, he will promise them something better than what they have and convince multitudes that it is in fact possible to get this "better." It will be his last act in time, and it will end with his eternal destruction in hell. Sadly, multitudes will go that way with him! Revelation describes this final act of deception and rebellion thus:

> *Now when the thousand years have expired, Satan will be released from his prison and will go out to deceive the nations which are in the four corners of the earth. Gog and Magog, to gather them together to battle, whose number is as the sand of the sea. They went up*

on the breadth of the earth and surrounded the camp of the saints and the beloved city. And fire came down from God out of heaven and devoured them. The devil, who deceived them, was cast into the lake of fire and brimstone where the beast and the false prophet are. And they will be tormented day and night forever and ever.

Revelation 20:7-10

THE MESSIANIC AGE

It must be borne in mind that millions of people, other than the Church, will enter the Messianic Age after the awful destructive events of the Day of the Lord (Zechariah 14:16). They will live in a near-perfect world and enjoy the righteous rule of Jesus over their lives. This will be from the present, but renovated and elevated, Jerusalem, but sadly they will still have sinful, carnal, and evil hearts! They will have to make a choice, just as we all had to, before the eternal state of God's Kingdom is ushered in. Those who steadfastly choose Christ and His reign will be transformed, their hearts will be "fixed," and they will become part of the "saved nations" living on a new Earth! Revelation 21:24 describes them in this way: "And the nations of those who are saved shall walk in its [the New Jerusalem's] light, and

the kings of the earth bring their glory and honor into it." These kings will not be part of the Church that will eternally dwell with Christ in the New Jerusalem and govern the new earth with Him.

The putting down of this final rebellion will set the stage for the Messianic Age to end and the new perfect order to be ushered in. This new order will be a new Earth, a new heavens, and the arrival of a "New Jerusalem" that will settle on the Earth! John saw this and described the unfolding vision of the city thus:

> *Now I saw a new heaven and a new earth, for the first heaven and the first earth had passed away. Also there was no more sea. Then I, John, saw the holy city, New Jerusalem, coming down out of heaven from God...*
>
> Revelation 21:1-2

The City Abraham saw and longed for will have finally arrived, and in it will be a mansion that Jesus personally built for every faithful, blood-washed, child of God (John 14:1-6)!

CHAPTER NINETEEN

A NEW HEAVEN AND A NEW EARTH

And behold, I am coming quickly, and My reward is with Me, to give to every one according to his work. I am the Alpha and the Omega, the Beginning and the End, the First and the Last.

Revelation 22:12-13

A CONTINUING CITY

A city populated by and governed by unregenerate people is a spawning ground for all manner of wickedness and evil. God is determined to pull them all down just as He did Sodom and Gomorrah. Indeed, He sets forth the overthrow of these two cities as an example and warning to all other cities (2 Peter 2:6; Jude

7). So the end of the age, amongst other things, will witness the cities of the Earth being torn down (Revelation 18:16-20; 16:18-19). We should take note of this.

However, though born in a garden, we are really made to dwell in a city. This city will be a continuing one, as it will be populated by holy people and governed by a holy God (Revelation 21:1-8)! Nothing evil or wicked or defiled will enter it or even put a foot near it (Revelation 22:15). The writer of the book of Hebrews acknowledges that we are looking for a permanent home since upon this Earth at present we have no continuing city (Hebrews 13:14). We are "pilgrims passing through," looking for a city that "has foundations, whose builder and maker is God" (Hebrews 11:8-10).

When our father Abraham went out from Ur of the Chaldeans in pursuit of God, he saw beyond the Promised Land to a city where the redeemed of all ages would dwell. This was his longing and desire! He wanted to dwell in the city of the living God (Hebrews 12:22). We too have this longing and expectation if we are rightly related to God through His Son, Jesus Christ.

THE HOME OF THE BRIDE

John has a spectacular vision of the New Jerusalem coming down from heaven to a renovated earth. It is the eternal home of the followers of Jesus. They are the Bride of Christ and they will weep no more and never experience pain again; all suffering will be a thing of the past (Revelation 21:4). They will be filled with indescribable joy as they mingle with saints and angels and see the face of Jesus every day. Echoing back to the second and third chapters of the Book, John hears an invitation to overcome, and thus inherit, all that God has planned for those who love Him. This will include a villa or mansion (Revelation 21:6-7).

The New Jerusalem is a real city and not a figurative description of the Church, as some would have us believe. Today we still speak about people as if they were cities. Actually Jesus did this Himself (Matthew 23:37-39) and political commentators and leaders often refer to leaders as cities. It is thus not unusual to hear them ask, "What does London, Paris, Moscow, or Washington have to say about this issue?" So people and cities are considered one and the same, but both exist, and when Scripture here refers to the New Jerusalem as the Bride of Christ, it is definitely not discounting the city's existence. The New Jerusalem is

real and the message is clear: the people of God, beautified by Christ, will inherit a city that will forever reflect their eternal brilliance. More than this, it will reflect the earthly foundation upon which God's plan of salvation was built, the Jewish people! Thus its twelve gates will be named after the twelve tribes of Israel, and its foundation stones will be inscribed with the names of the twelve Jewish Apostles of the Lamb (Revelation 21:12-14). Those who think that God is finished with the Jewish people are in for a rude awakening; they will live forever in a Jewish City! After all, Jesus said, "Salvation is of the Jews" (John 4:22).

THE GLORY OF THE CITY

The New Jerusalem that will come down from heaven and settle on a new Earth is a perfect cube. That is, it is fifteen hundred miles wide, high, and long. This is incredible and is beyond our ability to really appreciate. The new Earth will have no sea (Revelation 21:1), thus enabling such a magnificent structure to settle upon it. It is the eternal home of the children of God, and its glories are really indescribable, though John does attempt to give us a brilliant description of it. It sparkles with the beauty and brilliance of precious stones (Revelation 21:18-20), its

twelve gates are made from giant pearls (Revelation 21:21), and its streets are of pure gold (Revelation 21:21). The eyes of humankind have never seen anything like this before. It has no equal and never will, and it has one great theme: Jesus! He is the ultimate glory of the New Jerusalem. His presence, life, and glory will dominate the lives of all those who will eternally dwell there. The perfect Bride of Christ, redeemed and washed clean by His spilt blood, will forever adore Him, walk with Him on its streets of gold, and share in His governance of a kingdom that will eternally increase and have no end (Isaiah 9:6-7). This is why John recognized that all that God has prepared for us has not yet been revealed. He wrote:

> *Beloved, now we are children of God; and it has not yet been revealed what we shall be, but we know that when He is revealed, we shall be like Him, for we shall see Him as He is. And everyone who has this hope in Him purifies himself, just as He is pure.*
>
> 1 John 3:2-3

This in itself should cause us to "lean forward" to all that God by Jesus and through the power of the Holy Spirit is calling us to be and do for His Kingdom. We are

fools if we do not seek first the Kingdom of God and its righteousness. We all get "one shot" at the game of life, and we would do well to ensure that we make Jesus Lord. The "prize," as Paul put it, is amazing, but if the truth be known, only a few will claim it, for the great masses of humanity will reject God's love in Jesus and travel the broad road to destruction. Sadly, many on this broad road will travel it, though claiming to be followers of Jesus! They will hear Him say, "Many will say to Me in that day, 'Lord, Lord, have we not prophesied in Your name, cast out demons in Your name, and done many wonders in Your name?' And then I will declare to them, 'I never knew you; depart from Me, you who practice lawlessness!'" (Matthew 7:22-23).

John then notes that:

- Jesus will be the real foundation of the City (21:14).

- Jesus will be the focus of the City (21:22).

- Jesus will be the light of the City (21:23).

- Jesus will be the door to the City (21:27).

- Jesus will be the life of the City (22:1).

- Jesus will be the King of the City (22:3).

No wonder Jesus said that those who enter this eternal city will be blessed (Matthew 25:34). They will forever rejoice before God their Savior, having overcome not only the dictates of their carnal hearts but also the resistance and abuse of the world. Many will have "taken on the Beast" through history, as the early Church did and as the Sudanese Christians have today, and still more will remain steadfast as the final Beast enters the stage of history. All of this made them cling to Christ and seek His grace and cleansing even in death. The Spirit of God will watch over them. And a voice from heaven will declare,

> *"Blessed are the dead who die in the Lord from now on."*
>
> *"Yes," says the Spirit, "that they may rest from their labors, and their works follow them"*
>
> Revelation 14:13

THINGS TEMPORAL

FINAL WARNINGS AND EXHORTATIONS

"I, Jesus, have sent My angel to testify to you these things in the churches. I am the Root and the Offspring of David, the Bright and Morning Star."

Revelation 22:16

Once again, we are reminded that the whole Book of Revelation is for the whole Church. It is written to the churches as a warning of things to come, and it is unthinkable, as some erroneously teach, that the vast body of the book is irrelevant to the people of God! This deception has cleverly removed the book from Christian thinking and preaching and thereby, I believe, grieved the Spirit of God and left the Body of Christ ill-prepared

for what lies ahead. We must take very seriously the warning given in verses 18 and 19 of the last chapter:

> *For I testify to everyone who hears the words of the prophecy of this book: If anyone adds to these things God will add to him the plagues that are written in this book; and if anyone takes away from the words of the book of this prophecy, God shall take away his part from the Book of Life, from the holy city, and from the things which are written in this book.*
>
> Revelation 22:18-19

Strong words indeed, and worthy of noting!

FINAL EXHORTATIONS

As we noted at the beginning of this volume, the Book of Revelation is about the events that have to take place on Earth to make possible the second coming of Jesus. The Book is all about Him and His unveiling to His Church and to the world. All the players in this Book are fulfilling the purpose of God, even the Devil and the Beast (Revelation 17:17). These are "useful idiots" unwittingly setting the stage for Jesus to justly return to the earth, reward His people, judge His enemies, and rule in righteousness. The

Book is about His triumph over all that is evil and wicked and is thus a great blessing and encouragement to all those who take the time to read and study it. We have done just this, and remember that God promises to spiritually enrich the lives of those who do so (Revelation 1:3).

The final chapter "speaks into our present" and lays much stress upon the second coming of Jesus. However, in looking for His second coming we must hold all the things in this Book close to our hearts. Jesus says in verse 7, "Behold, I am coming quickly! Blessed is he who keeps the words of the prophecy of this book." In verse 12 He reminds us that when He comes it will be to judge His people and reward them for the nature of their service and commitment to Him, and in verse 16 He reminds us that He wants His Church to know all the teaching of this Book. Most of all, He wants them to know His Jewish lineage and that He is returning to the world as the King of the Jews! He will sit on David's great throne and finally fulfill all the wonderful promises that God made to Israel. He will return to a Jewish Jerusalem (Matthew 23:37-39).

Jesus expects His Church to be watchful and excited about His second coming. There should be something in us that longs for His appearing (Titus 2:11-15), and therefore as we walk with Him daily, "the Spirit and the bride say,

'Come!' And let him who hears say, 'Come!'" Those thirsty for life, can come and drink freely of the water of life. Jesus invites us all to love Him, walk with Him, and look for His appearing, because He is coming sooner than you think!

EVEN SO, COME, LORD JESUS!

MALCOLM
HEDDING

Malcolm Hedding is an Ordained Assemblies of God minister and church planter, starting many churches throughout South Africa from 1975 - 2000. Malcolm is a tried and proven leader of local congregations, bringing to his ministry a unique understanding of local church life.

Currently Malcolm serves as one of the Associate Pastors of World Outreach Church in Murfreesboro, Tennessee. He is considered a leading theologian in the Christian Zionist world today. His many years of involvement in this sphere, beginning in 1976, have earned him much respect and the esteem of his peers within the Jewish and Christian world.

He is an acclaimed International speaker on Israel and the Church in these crucial and challenging times. Malcolm travels extensively, revitalizing the Church in terms of its role in these days. Given his unique and vast speaking forums around the globe, Malcolm has a view and understanding of the Body of Christ that few get or have. He has published several books on Prayer, the Book of Revelation, Understanding Israel and a foundational series on Biblical Christian Zionism that has been translated into German, Finnish, Nepalese and Mandarin. He is a prolific writer and regularly contributes to magazines and papers of various types including the Jerusalem Post, the Christian Edition. Malcolm is also asked to speak regularly on radio shows and Christian broadcasting Networks.

Malcolm holds a Bachelor in Theology degree and two diplomas in Theology. He is a dedicated servant of Christ and seeks to glorify Him in all that he does.